CREATIVE WRITING CAREER

Becoming a Writer of Movies, Video Games, and Books

Justin M. Sloan

Cover Art by Norman Felchle

ISBN: 1503125831
ISBN-13: 978-1503125834

Acknowledgements

Above all I must thank my wife Ugulay, and our children Verona and Brendan, for their love and patience as I spent hours at the computer to put this together. They, and our third child that we plan to have someday, inspire me and have encouraged me every step of the way, in this endeavor and with my fiction writing and screenplays. I love you all and cannot imagine life without you. Next, I would like to thank my mother, father, sister and brother, as well as my other family and friends. I am surrounded by positive people who believe in me. I have never had any naysayers, and for that I appreciate you all.

My instructors at the Johns Hopkins University MA in writing program and at the University of California, Los Angeles School of Theater, Film, and Television were amazing and incredibly valuable to my life and to building the content that became this book. The same goes for my critique groups, editors, and beta readers used for this and other books.

I would like to thank all interviewees who agreed to let me include them in this book, and Stephan Bugaj in particular for his kind foreword and the incredibly important role he has played in my creative career. I would like to thank my current employer for giving me a chance to pursue my dreams as a writer, and all of you for caring enough to be a part of my dream by reading this book. You are amazing, and for you I continue on.

CONTENTS

FOREWORD, BY STEPHAN BUGAJ

When Justin approached me to be interviewed for and write the foreword to his book, the first question I asked myself was: "why does the world need another writing career advice book?" I realized the answer was threefold:

1) All careers in all industries are constantly shifting so new advice must be distributed that keeps up with the changing times.

2) Telling aspirants and newbies how right our perspectives on writing craft and business are is a major source of entertainment for writers – and don't we have as much right to amusement as anyone else?

3) And finally, most importantly, while most career advice books are edited by someone who broke in a million years ago, Justin was coming at this from the fresh perspective of assembling advice from people who had been useful during his very recent breaking-in process.

New writers are faced with a sea of choices when it comes to writing career advice guides, and the fact that Justin was putting together a book that would take his readers through what he had just gone through seemed like a very good idea. Justin is also bringing his military background to bear with his Veterans Writing Project interviews in Part Six and in his next book devoted to helping ex-military who want to break into the entertainment industry, and I am very supportive of any effort to help ex-servicemembers find their next careers.

Justin's fresh perspective practically guarantees his book being pragmatic and sensibly optimistic, rather than the usual bitter and cynical advice books from more seasoned and beleaguered writers. While it's important to know what the perils and pitfalls of a writing career are, when you're getting started out it's equally useful to hear about things that actually can work, and be encouraged that there is the possibility of a professional career in writing if you approach it sensibly and practically.

Pragmatism and hard work are indeed the key to writing success. I am friends with a number of very successful, A-list screenwriters and they all are pragmatists with a strong work ethic—starry-eyed dreamers and indulgent artistes don't survive in the commercial writing business (there are rare exceptions, but if you're one of those you're not reading this book, anyway).

Pairing Justin's own insights with interviews also seemed like a great way to broaden and balance the book by including the perspectives of people with different experience and expertise. So I decided to contribute this foreword and an interview because Justin's book provides a fresh perspective and an up-to-date practical approach to building a professional writing career put together by someone who just did that, successfully.

And he did so using the tools of our times: politely and professionally reaching-out to people in the business via e-mail and social networking sites, blogging for exposure, and ultimately taking a job writing in one of the most contemporary of writing media – video games.

In fact, Justin and I "met" online, through LinkedIn. He found me because of my blog at www.bugaj.com and my *Pixar's 22 Rules of Story, Analyzed eBook,* and approached me very politely for advice about a writing career. Having gone from tech artist to screenwriter at Pixar was a monumentally difficult achievement, but that alone would not have qualified me to give anyone any career advice (it's too unique a situation). But since I'd also gone through the UCLA professional program, optioned a few indie features into development hell, and accumulated a massive enough collection of rejections and failed "sure things" to be considered a "real writer," I decided I wouldn't be harming anyone by giving them a wee bit of career advice. So we corresponded.

Because Justin was intelligent and pleasant to deal with online, when I was hiring writers and saw his resume and samples come through, those got read immediately. You can cynically call every producer, publisher and executive's preference for hiring people they know cronyism or cliquishness if you like, but this is a relationship business because creation is too difficult, personal and time consuming to try to do it with incompatible people. Being a good person to work with is as essential as being a good writer.

So Justin's insights into how to present and comport yourself in order to break-in have been recently successful, and how you "sell yourself" is one of the most crucial aspects of breaking into the industry. The only possibly more important aspect is how great your stories are. Maybe more important, but then again many publishers and producers would much rather work with a pleasant hack than a petulant genius – so if you can learn to be a pleasant genius, success!

In other words, professionalism, politeness and honesty are utterly essential to this process, and since I hired Justin, I know that he has those qualities, and I know his book will inspire them in its readers both by instruction and example.

As for the craft side, Justin (and several of the writers he interviews in this book) proved their knowledge and skill to me in the form of samples, interview responses, and lectures. I was glad to see how many writers I know and have worked with were willing to share their knowledge with the community. They're all good people you can learn from.

What this book covers in terms of craft won't be radically different from other, more in-depth books, as is the nature of overview books; but it will provide you with some new perspectives on those ideas, and allow the book to serve as a single-source overall guide to a writing career that can then be augmented with more specialized and in-depth craft books and/or experiential learning.

So read this book now. Right now! It is timely and relevant, and therefore useful. It will help you in your quest to become a professional writer. No book can make that journey for you, but this is one that can serve as a helpful guide along the way.

Stephan Vladimir Bugaj

Los Angeles, CA

INTRODUCTION

Since starting my job as a writer of video games, and even before as a novelist and freelance screenwriter, I have been asked over and over how I became a writer and what my advice would be for aspiring writers. It seems everyone wants to be a writer, and they want to know what they can do to make that dream come true. However, most people do not understand how to position themselves to be ready when presented with an opportunity. The good news is that there are a multitude of books out there on the writing craft, as well as many events and educational programs. You can become a writer, but you must have the discipline and passion.

The not-so-good news is that you cannot exactly plan your big breakthrough into the life of writing, so you have to exhibit an extreme amount of patience. When I was trying to make it as a writer, I had a writer friend who constantly reminded me to focus on patience and wisdom: patience in terms of waiting for my chance, and wisdom in the sense that I had to do everything possible to be ready when my chance came. Now it is your turn to learn patience and wisdom, so that you too can achieve the dream.

Creative Writing Career: Becoming a Writer of Movies, Video Games, and Books explores how to prepare for a career as a writer. The book includes instruction on the process and ways to improve one's craft, but mostly focuses on how to be discovered and where to concentrate energy in the meantime. The content is supplemented by writer interviews, featuring some incredibly gifted people who share the wisdom they have gained. As with writing and most aspects of life, I have chosen to rely on those with demonstrated wisdom to move ahead. This book presents that wisdom for the reader to do the same. The book is laid out as follows:

PART ONE: GETTING STARTED

Too many aspiring writers try to find careers in creative writing without having properly positioned themselves for such careers. Here I describe four ways you can position yourself, ways that include improving your craft, networking, ensuring you are discoverable, and building up your credibility. The next section stresses the importance of staying focused on your passion. Finally in Part One we discuss inspiration for a writer and the importance of finding a place to write.

Part One includes an interview with Allen Warner, who has written comics, video games, and film, and who shares his experience working across the medium of our focus. Next we speak with Tomiko Breland, a freelance editor and associate publisher with the independent publisher Zharmae. Tomiko shares her thoughts on freelancing and what she looks for when deciding whether to take on a book. The final interview of Part one is with Bruce Spiegelman, who discusses how he successfully sold several independent screenplays and saw his words come to life on the screen.

PART TWO: LEARNING TO WRITE

When you are starting to learn to write, consider the multitude of paths available, such as writing classes, conferences, or critique groups. Read the interviews at the end of each part of this book to see how others have learned the craft and how they continue to improve it. After you read Part Two, prepare a plan for yourself on how you can take your craft to the next level. We start this section by examining writing programs and laying out two programs as case studies of what you can hope to attain from a writing program: the Johns Hopkins University (JHU) MA in writing and the University of California, Los Angeles (UCLA) program in screenwriting. Next we discuss the workings of a writing group and how to find one (or create your own), and how members of a writing group should help each other along the writing journey. Finally in Part Two we examine the considerations that go into developing your characters, as well as a method for character creation. The work must be done, because if you do not care enough about your characters to get to know them, then why should your readers?

Part Two includes an interview with Will Wight, the successful self-published author of the *Traveler's Gate* trilogy. Next we speak with the award-winning writer and director of the short film *1982*, Jeremy Breslau, who discusses his time at film school and his transition to writing video games. The final interview of Part Two presents Joyce Lee, a novelist and filmmaker, to hear her view on the creative process and hurdles women face in the entertainment industry.

PART THREE: STORY STRUCTURE

Although my goal is not to teach you the craft of writing, all writers should have a basic understanding of story structure. Therefore, Section Three describes the main story structure methods so that you may make an educated decision on which to use, or to at least know why you decide to avoid them. The three main types of structure that people talk about are laid here and are *Save the Cat, The Writer's Journey*, and *The Sequence Approach*. Lastly is a structure that is not so common in my circles, but that may have something to offer you, which is called the "Seven Point Story Structure." These sections include my story *Teddy Bears in Monsterland* as an example, to see how the structures are applied.

In this section we speak with Bob Saenz about his experience with screenwriting outside of LA and hear about his writing style and his thoughts on structure. Next we speak with Chris Jalufka, a screenwriter and artist who runs the EvilTender.com website, has years of experience as a professional screenplay reader, and has strong opinions about books on structure. As the structure books are highly skewed toward screenwriting, I chose two screenwriters for this section. However, the advice in the structure books and from these two writers is applicable across media.

PART FOUR: SCREENWRITERS

Part Four focuses on how screenwriters in particular should approach positioning themselves for a career. We start by presenting different paths for breaking into screenwriting and examines the screenwriting books and podcasts aspiring screenwriters should read and listen to. Next we assess the top contests and the value of both entering and resubmitting to such contests. We learn through my experience with my first short film and explore the process of putting a short film together. I present "Pixar's 22 Rules of Story" and make the argument for both knowing the so-called rules and reading Stephan Bugaj's free e-book, *Pixar's 22 Rules of Story, Analyzed*. Lastly in Part Four we study several of the top screenwriting conferences and look to the Austin Film Festival and Writers Guild Foundation events as case studies to observe the proper etiquette and strategy for attending such events.

Part Four is packed full of interviews with screenwriters, with experience ranging from the beginning stages to the more advanced. We present an interview with Stephan Bugaj, where we learn from his twelve years at Pixar, his time as Creative Development Director at a video game company, and his writing now that he has relocated to LA. Next, Mark Simborg shares his advice on finding literary management and the first steps of success with television specs. Finally in this section, Paul Zeidman discusses his success through the Black List, a resource all screenwriters must be aware of.

PART FIVE: VIDEO GAME WRITERS

Part Five focuses on how video game writers in particular should approach positioning themselves for a career in writing. The section starts by examining what makes video games work, and what games an aspiring video game writer should be playing. Next we examine the types of writing jobs in the game industry, and what learning opportunities are available. This is followed up by a look at the Game Developers Conference, focusing on what classes the conference hosts for writers and designers.

Part Five presents an interview with Anthony Burch, the lead writer on *Borderlands 2*, for his take on the industry and being discovered from his webseries and online game critiques. Next we speak with Joshua Rubin, a veteran of Hollywood and the video game industry, to discuss how he left the world of film and television and went on to win an award for his writing on *Assassins Creed II*, then move on to *Destiny*, and now writes for the video game version of *Game of Thrones*. We finish this section by talking with Matthew Ritter about his graphic novels and how his side projects led him to a job working on *The Walking Dead* and *Tales from the Borderlands*.

PART SIX: FICTION AND NON-FICTION AUTHORS

Part Six focuses on how authors of fiction and non-fiction books in particular should approach positioning themselves for a writing career. Here we look at some ways to stay engaged through writing conferences, critique groups, writing classes, and blogs. Next we explore some of my favorite books on writing for novels and creative non-fiction, which include *Reading Like a Writer and How Fiction Works*. We review processes for publishing, such as which literary magazines are in what tier of submissions, niche publishing, small presses, resources such as *Poets & Writers*, and the option of self-publishing. Lastly, Part Six presents such writing conferences as the San Francisco Writers Conference (SFWC), Litquake, The Association of Writers & Writing Programs (AWP), and includes a section on an SFWC-sponsored event titled "Women Writing in the Redwoods."

We start this section's interviews with Kelly Ann Jacobson, who shares her experience publishing her first two novels and her advice for aspiring writers hoping to publish their first work. We speak with Laura Hedgecock about writing non-fiction and her book about learning to capture life's moments in written form. Next we speak with Ron Capps, the founder of the Veterans Writing Project, and discuss his non-fiction book and writing opportunities for military veterans. Our final interview in the book is with Jerri Bell, Managing Editor of the literary publication *O-Dark-Thirty*, to discuss her experience as an editor.

CONCLUSION

Having shared my advice on how to position yourself for a career in creative writing, as well as the advice of my fellow writers, the book concludes with a challenge for the reader to lay out a writing career plan.

As a disclaimer I should state that this book is not meant to be authoritative or comprehensive; it is simply a guide to help you. Think of me as a mentor and friend, here to provide guidance as you begin your journey. I am not an expert. I am one guy who has had several careers, which have included the Marines, the U.S. Government, and the banking sector. I left these careers and now successfully work full-time as a writer, and many of the people I interviewed have had similar paths. When you too leave the rat race and have a career in writing that you look forward to every day, please write me and let me know. I love hearing success stories and anxiously await hearing yours.

If you would like a free PDF to print for your writing career plan, email me at SloanArtist@gmail.com with the subject line "Writing Career Plan." Likewise, if you are a military veteran or interested in programs for veterans, keep your eyes open for my upcoming book, *Veterans in Creative Careers*. As a bonus, if you email me at SloanArtist@gmail.com with the subject line "Veterans in Creative Careers," I will send you a PDF with Veteran writing program information and interviews. These will serve as chapters in the final book.

PART ONE: GETTING STARTED

Position Yourself to Become a Full-Time Writer

How many times have we wondered about the amount of luck required to make it as a writer? Take a cue from Peter Dinklage's recent words on luck: "Saying I was lucky negates the hard work I put in and spits on that guy who's freezing his ass off back in Brooklyn."[1]

To make it in this world, you must position yourself to be fortunate. Relying on luck, or attributing your success to luck, is a mistake. If you are not putting in the sweat and tears to make it happen, you will need a whole heck of a lot of luck, and even that may not save you. Do the work to obtain your dreams. Instead of luck, let's hope to be fortunate and be bold enough to make it so.

I want to share with you what I did that I believe helped put me in the right place at the right time, as well as what many of us are doing to position ourselves for creative writing careers. Some of you may not want to write for video games, but I hope my advice is useful for all writers in search of a full-time job that caters to your passion for writing. It may give you hope to know that I am also a screenwriter and novelist. To make it as a writer, I would stress the following four pieces of advice:

1. It's all about the craft. Well, maybe not exactly, but if you

---

[1] The Objective Standard, "Peter Dinklage: 'I Hate that Word, 'Lucky,'" August 24, 2013, http://www.theobjectivestandard.com/2013/08/peter-dinklage-i-hate-that-word-lucky/.

do not focus on improving your craft to its finest, no one is going to hire you. Perhaps my interviewers for my current job did not think my writing was perfect, but they could tell that I was (and am) dedicated to improving my craft, had already put in many hours of writing and learning, and will continue to be passionate about writing. Take classes, attend workshops, start a critique group, and maybe get a certificate or degree in writing. Start a blog about writing. I am certain all of this helped in my case, and will discuss these points in the pages that follow. In the end it mostly comes down to craft.

2. Put yourself out there. Networking should come into play, but only if you are spending the maximum time possible on your craft. If you are out there meeting folks all the time and saying what a great writer you are, but you are not writing, then you are not a writer. Instead, go home and write. If you are passionate about writing, have actually been writing, and are ready for that next step—then get out there and meet people. Attend the San Francisco Writers Conference, the Austin Film Festival, a Writers Guild Foundation event, the Game Developers Conference, or a writing event at a local university. Meet people and discuss your interests and passions. This does not necessarily have to be face to face, as you can connect with writers online through LinkedIn or forums such as DoneDealPro. I am not positive that networking helped me to land my writing job, but I know it helped me to meet people who gave me advice about the craft and how to position myself for the job. If I had not met them, it would have not been likely for my current career to happen. So go out there and meet people. It may encourage you to know that Ashley Miller (*Thor; X-Men First Class*) met his writing partner in an online forum. Maybe you will as well.

3. Make sure people can find you. You do not want to be the one always trying to find people to connect with, so make sure others can find you online. Build a website that lists what you are working on, and maybe include a writing resume. Update your LinkedIn profile to cater to what you want to do. You are your product. Create a profile to stand out. About six months ago I made my LinkedIn profile and web presence all about writing and entertainment (I included my acting and storyboarding as well). My LinkedIn profile is certainly not the best profile ever, but I have noticed an increase in traffic in the past six months, and getting noticed like this definitely increases my chances in the business. View my profile for some ideas on how to present yourself as a writer, and feel free to send me an invitation to connect while you are there.

4. Build some credibility. I advise doing whatever you can to build up your resume and LinkedIn profile. Some writers will say that none of that matters, because it is all about your writing samples. However, a lot of those same writers will not even look at what you have written for your sample if you have nothing to your name. Like your story needs a hook, so too do you. When you say you have interned at Benderspink (screenwriting), Folio Literary Management (fiction), or Telltale Games (video games), they will be more likely to take you seriously. Likewise if you are trying to reach out to people on LinkedIn. Make your LinkedIn profile and personal website your calling cards. Ensure your web presence tells the story of who you want to be.

You are never too old or too busy to pursue new passions. With a job, in the midst of working on my second masters, and with a 16-month-old daughter, I interned with a literary magazine and then a literary management company; both were amazing experiences. Taking on writing work is always possible. Look up what internships will allow you to work remotely and assess for yourself how many hours per week you think it will take. You may even learn something. Other opportunities include reading for contests like the Austin Film Festival screenplay contest, or reading for local literary magazines. If you live in the Bay Area, see Zoetrope's *All Story* literary magazine for a reading opportunity. Get out there and explore the possibilities.

To reiterate, you must learn how to write, practice your craft, network through conferences and other in-person avenues, network online, build up your resume, show off your resume via LinkedIn and your author website, and continue to learn through reading and possibly through internships. You can always do more, but for now, I hope this helps you to get started.

Avoid Distractions

In my quest to become a full-time writer, I thought I would try all sorts of methods, including applying for other jobs in the industry such as production or storyboard art positions. This may have helped me in some ways, but I learned that being focused is what really pays off. I would advise you all to try what you must, but never lose sight of your goal of being a writer. I hope the following is helpful for those of you that may have considered other ways to break into the industry.

During my search for any sort of job related to the entertainment industry, I contacted people in publishing, video games, and film, asking them to meet for coffee. Several such meetings were with higher-ups at some of Hollywood's top animation companies. Though being told that I could get a job with them was nice, and many of the people I met with highly encouraged me to consider going for such a job, I am glad I did not go that route. My take-away from these meetings was that if I want to be a writer, I should focus on writing.

The message to stay focused did not sink in right away, and I spent a lot of time and money not listening to the advice I'm giving you now. My lack of focus started with me meeting some storyboard artists at the Austin Film Festival, one of whom went on to become a writer at Disney. I learned that transitioning from storyboard artist to writer is common in these animation companies. Since I had always been a bit of an artist, I thought that pursuing a career as a storyboard artist could be the right path for me to break in to the industry and one day become a writer. I storyboarded my own short film and figured this made sense.

The next step was to join storyboard groups on LinkedIn, which provided very useful feedback. I took a Skillshare.com class taught by a Disney storyboard artist, then a class at the Animation Collaborative taught by a Pixar storyboard artist. Through this process I learned about storyboarding specifically, but I also improved my storytelling ability and increased my knowledge of film and blocking.

However, I also learned that storyboarding can use up an incredible amount of time. This is what led me to the conclusion that I was wasting time on a distraction. I told myself to stay focused on writing, and I hope you can learn from my mistake. This is not to say that studying storyboard art is a mistake, as it was an excellent learning experience. However, it may have been a mistake to become involved in projects that used so much of my time, time that I could have been using to write a screenplay or novel instead.

As with storyboarding, or production—or whatever it is that takes up your time—if you want to be a writer, you should be focused on becoming a better writer. Dedicate some time to your other interests and hobbies, but only if doing so allows you time to feel fulfilled as a writer.

I buckled down and focused on writing and improving my craft. I found a writing partner, interned at Folio Literary Management part time, and networked like crazy.

If your goal is to simply break into the industry, go with whatever opportunities you can find. But if this is the case, you should probably not be focused on a career as a writer anyway; writers write out of a passion for writing. How are you going to compete with someone who eats and breathes this stuff? Likewise, how are you as a writer going to compete with someone who eats and breathes production or story art? Or finance? Or whatever it is you are doing, getting sidetracked, when you should be putting as much of yourself as you can into writing?

If you feel this passion for writing, then focus and go write.

Find Inspiration to Write

We all find ways to inspire our writing. For me, it is often a location. I am especially partial to a quaint café, a local Starbucks, or a bar with a dreamy ambiance. Most of all I find places that inspire memories and a sense of nostalgia to be the best writing environments.

Recently I traveled to Washington, D.C., where I had lived for five years before moving to the San Francisco Bay Area. We were there to help my sister-in-law as she had her first baby, which meant I was in charge of watching my seventeen-month-old daughter while my wife helped her sister, and my time for writing was scarce. However, I was fortunate enough to escape and write for a few hours at the Tabard Inn. Right away I knew I had found my writing location. I settled in at the Tabard Inn from the moment I arrived, and two hours later I had busted out what I believe was some of my best writing that year.

The Tabard Inn brought back memories that helped me get in a creative mindset. I remembered my second year of graduate school in D.C. and the friends and experiences there. I thought about my time working for the government, and remembered all of the fun interagency conflict that my work had entailed. The inn also brought back memories of meeting my wife, falling in love (almost instantly), and proposing to her. I have had some great times in D.C., and as I sat there in the dimly lit lounge, full of couches and a soft flickering of candlelight, I drank my coffee stout and felt the muse sweep over me. Whenever I return to D.C., I know where I will be writing.

I share this to encourage you all to go out there and find what it is that inspires you to write at your best. Is it a dark lounge, or a crowded Starbucks? Some people like libraries, but such places are too quiet for me. For me, hidden gems like the Tabard Inn work best. But these gems do not only exist in places we have been before. Just as inspiring as the familiar inn that evokes vivid memories can be those new places that fill us with a sense of mystery.

If you have traveled abroad and are a writer, I am sure you have found many great places to write. I have lived in Japan, Italy, and Korea, and traveled extensively beyond these locations as well. If you get a chance to visit the pastel-walled location of Cinque Terre in Italy, you will probably want to sit and look out over the ocean cliffs and write the next bestselling novel (during breaks from hiking between villages and exploring the unbelievable scenery, that is.) Here is some golden advice for you if you do make it to Italy: I believe the path for the "nature beach" (read nude beach) is just off of the fourth trail. When is the last time you wrote naked on a beach? Bring some fresh pesto and a bottle of wine and you have heaven (unless you forget your sunblock). I may or may not have done this; but my screenplay *Hounds of God* (soon to be a novel) has several scenes directly inspired from Cinque Terre, and every time I read the script I am whisked back to that wonderful place.

How about the temples in Japan? I am sure you will be inspired as the rain sends ripples through the pond that surrounds the golden temple of Kinkakuji. Don't forget the tranquil beaches of Okinawa and the sake-pineapple bread that you must try, if you ever visit the pineapple brewery there. Then there are the endless beer gardens that fill Sapporo in the summers. Japan, like many countries in this great world, is full of culture and architecture sure to inspire you. I have a novel outlined and a screenplay completed that were both heavily inspired by my travels in Japan. Writing these stories and remembering everything I experienced over there was an amazing experience. A trip you take to such a place may be purely for fun now, but the memories will likely find their way into your writing someday.

So many places have inspired my writing or served as perfect writing locations. I recall a bar in Germany that felt like a medieval tavern, a hotel in Puerto Rico that was surrounded by rainforest (which made me fear for my life as I wondered how long it would take someone to find my body if the worst should happen), and castles and battlefields in Scotland that directly inspired certain chapters of my novels. If not for these experiences, I would not be the writer I am today or plan to be in the future.

Get out and see the world; or at least find the amazing café, bar, or castle in your backyard that will bring out your best writing. Read my co-blogger John Kingston's post "On Solitude and Writing" (http://redwoodssociety.com/seclusion-writing/) for his related experience (spoiler alert: it has to do with a week in a cabin.) Do whatever it takes and get out there! You can write at Starbucks or in your house every day, and maybe that will be all you need. But I choose a more inspiring path, and encourage you to do the same.

Part One Next Steps

In this first chapter we discussed how to position yourself and what to do to set yourself up to be a writer, so let's start with creating an early draft writing career plan. In this plan I want you to think about how much writing you hope to accomplish over the next year and then over the next five years, and what you plan on doing with your final products (submitting to managers and agents, self-publishing, or going the small press route). Include where you would like to be as a writer in one year from now and then in five years from now. Do you want to be a full-time author? Work as a writer at a video game company? Make millions every day? Put it in that plan, even if it is more of a dream. What do you plan on doing to get you there? Prioritize this list based on what you can do immediately and realistically. What have you already done, and how can you leverage these experiences? Include as much as you can in this initial plan, and really give it some thought. Extra credit for making a goal list and hanging it on the wall next to your desk. At the end of the book I will ask you to update this career plan, so keep it in mind as you read. Write your plan in narrative format. To get started, consider the following questions:

My Writing Plan

1. How much writing do you hope to accomplish over the next year? Over the next five years?

2. What will you do with your final product over the next year? Over the next five years?

3. Where do you want to end up in the next year? In the next five years?

4. What else can you do to get there over the next year? Over the next five years?

Interview: Allen Warner, Multimedia Writer

With each great film comes great writing. And sometimes that great writing comes from a Bay Area screenwriter. Below you will find my interview with Allen Warner, a writer of comics, games, and movies. Allen Warner co-wrote the script for the upcoming animated film, The Tale of the Seas. He co-created and wrote the popular comic book series *Ninja Boy*, which was published by DC Comics, and optioned by Warner Bros. Animation. He's written for DC Comics since 2001, co-creating the series Skye Runner, and The New Dynamix, and wrote stories for the Wildstorm Winter Special, DC Comics Presents Wildstorm, and the *Ninja Boy: Faded Dreams* graphic novel. He's worked as a video game writer for studios including TinyCo, Circle 5 Studios, and Dreamslair Entertainment, and is currently working on an unannounced video game project, and an upcoming comic book series for BOOM! Studios. His experience is very relevant to this book because he started by involving himself in projects across the multiple forms of media.

***

Justin Sloan: Allen, thank you for making time to speak with us about your writing experience, and about your latest film, *The Tale of the Seas*.[2] You have some great experience with comics and games. How did you get into writing and specifically these projects?

Allen Warner: Thanks Justin. I've been writing as long as I can remember, but I got started professionally back in 2000. My longtime friend and collaborator Alé Garza had drawn an awesome image for an idea he had called *Ninja Boy*. It grabbed

---

[2] Film Website: http://thetaleoftheseas.com/; Facebook link: www.facebook.com/thetaleoftheseas

the attention of an agent at a comic convention who wanted to know if he'd be interested in pitching it as a cartoon. Alé had some ideas for names and scenes and the basic story, but hadn't fleshed it all out, so he asked me to come on to help him fully plot it out, and bring it to life. I wrote a pretty detailed synopsis of the world, backstory, characters, plot, etc., and we bounced it back and forth until we were both happy with it. The whole experience of initially showing it to the agent and taking it to different studios is a story in and of itself, but the end result was that it got optioned by Warner Bros. Animation. Alé had previously worked for a comic company called Wildstorm Studios, and we'd always wanted to do it as a comic too, so we pitched it to them. They had me write a short story for an anthology book they had going at the time as a sort of tryout, and when that went well, we got the green light, and they published *Ninja Boy* as a series.

That got my foot in the door in comics, but, just as importantly, I met a bunch of really talented artists who worked for the studio, and when they needed help with something on the writing side, they would hit me up, and vice versa. Those connections led to a bunch of cool published and unpublished stories, a lot of good times, and some great friendships.

I didn't really know anyone working in games, or at least not anyone in a position to help me get a job, but I've always been a gamer, and always wanted to write for games, so I just started reaching out to companies however I could. Some recruiters and producers contacted me, but honestly, most of my video game work has come via LinkedIn. I'd connect with people in a position to hire me, and send them a really brief message asking them to get in touch if they were ever looking for a writer. It led to a lot of "Sure. Will Do," responses, but also led to a lot of interviews, tryouts, and immediate work.

JS: That is wonderful that LinkedIn has worked so well for you—I can certainly attribute much of my career to networking through LinkedIn as well, and would advise

other writers to take advantage of that and other social media. What would be your advice for new writers looking to be involved in such projects?

AW: The advice everyone gives that is absolutely true is that you should write as much, and read as much, as you possibly can. Like everything else, the more you write, the better you get, and the more you find your own voice. When you read other people's work, or watch and break it down in a game or movie, you can take the techniques you love, and try to avoid the things you don't. You eventually, and continually—because it never really ends—find what works for you, and then just hope that other people like what you're doing as much as you do. You have to write for yourself at the end of the day, because opinions differ, and it makes the inevitable rejection a lot easier to swallow.

My main advice, through experience, is to finish. And when you finish, show it to people. It applies to writing, but really everything creative. I've known way too many people, including myself, who have a great idea for something but for one reason or another find a reason not to finish. The reasons are oftentimes legitimate, but that's irrelevant. People, and especially people in charge of getting things produced, respond to fully realized ideas and, ideally, tangible product. You have an infinitely better chance of selling something, or selling yourself, by showing a complete project you've created. If it's finished. You might still get rejected, and you probably will, but at least you can take solace in the fact that you've done something and move on to the next opportunity. Rejection sucks, but if all you have are a bunch of ideas in your head, or your note-book, or your computer, you don't even have a chance to get rejected.

More specifically, if you want to break into comics and games, you need to connect with people who are in comics and games. I'm pretty bad at social media, but that's a great place to start. Conventions are even better. Contact people who work in the industry you want to work in, both established big names, and hungry up-and-comers like you. Let them know what you're about. If they're the least bit responsive, show them your best completed project. For comics and games, I'm a big believer in finding artists, programmers, etc., basically anyone who doesn't classify themselves as writers. In my experience, almost everyone has an idea for a story, but either doesn't have the time, discipline, or ability to write it. Offer up your services. Hopefully for a fee, but if it's the right person and scenario, do it for free just to get your name out there and make them, and other professionals, aware of your existence. It's all a learning experience, and even if the project never manifests, the exposure to one professional can build your resume and hopefully snowball into something bigger.

JS: You really do have to finish projects to be taken seriously as a writer. Now that you have some experience and connections, do you find that people tend to come to you? How much of what you work on comes from you as the originator?

AW: For most of my published work, I've collaborated with an artist or company to build on an idea they already have, flesh it out, and add my point of view to it. I really enjoy the back-and-forth, and I feel like the most successful projects I've been involved in have been with people who are open and humble enough to let go a little and embrace new ideas for the overall story. This goes for myself as well, working with some really creative people and great editors who've given notes that I might have initially rejected, but we worked together to create something better and different than I could have come up with on my own. It's easy to get locked into your own ideas when you sit alone for hours staring at a computer screen, and even easier to get angry when someone wants you to change or delete something you spent all those hours working on. You have to be true to yourself, but you have to always be open to other ideas. Finding the way to the best story possible is all that matters.

That being said, I started writing screenplays because I didn't want to be dependent on other people to see something to completion. When you collaborate, you can easily get lost in that circle of back-and-forth, lose your momentum, and never finish. Screenplays allowed me to tell a whole story exactly the way I wanted to tell it, and after I was finished I could call on other people to read it and give me their feedback. And every single script I've written is better for incorporating someone else's feedback. Those completed screenplays may never become films, but they've served as comic pitches, video game work samples, and, at the very least, they look pretty good on my bookshelf.

JS: I actually got my job as a video game writer with a sitcom pilot as my writing sample, so you never know what project will help you and how. But let's move on to the main point of our interview, which is to discuss your work in *The Tale of the Seas*. What was it about this project that made you want to be involved and kept you excited?

AW: Well, first I saw the concept art, and it was incredible. I got super excited, and that was pretty much it. I also loved the idea of writing something that was kid-friendly because I have a young son, and honestly, my mind usually doesn't immediately go to those types of stories, so I also loved the idea that I wouldn't have to wait until he was thirteen to show him something I wrote. When I got to read the initial script, I was all the way sold. It was heartfelt, and poignant, and timely, and funny, and had a dark fantasy feel that I've loved since I was a kid, with movies like *The Dark Crystal*, *The Secret of Nimh*, *The Black Cauldron*, and so many others. Knowing that I was getting paid to write a movie that would actually get made didn't hurt either.

JS: I am right there with you in wanting to have something developed that I can show my children, and want to

congratulate you again on achieving that with *The Tale of the Seas*. Can you share some more information about how you got involved in this project?

AW: Yoram Benz, the founder and creative director for an awesome animation studio called One Eyed Robot, contacted me. He'd already written a script, but wanted to have someone else take a look at it, and add their two cents. He was immediately open to changes and additions, and was really responsive when I sent him my ideas. He gave me a great amount of trust and leeway to build on his initial story, and create something new. He had great feedback on the changes I made, allowed me rewrite almost all the dialogue, and added even more great ideas after my hack at it to make the final draft really shine.

JS: The film looks stunning and touching. I am curious to hear what you think it is about the film that draws in its audience and makes them care, and how you dealt with this as a writer.

AW: Yoram and his team at One Eyed Robot really deserve all the credit for that, along with the score and sound design by Marcus Fischer. I think we're so used to the huge-budget, super-polished, sometimes-generic look of feature animated films nowadays that seeing something like the trailer they created hits a nerve. It's different. It feels more homegrown and heartfelt, but still is clearly crafted by talented professionals. A lot of animated films are formulaic and silly, but I think they did an amazing job in the trailer showing that this movie is neither of those. Like the examples I named above, it's a kids' movie that isn't afraid to touch on adult subjects, and isn't afraid to go dark. I think we underestimate kids' ability to process more serious subject matter, so we respond positively to something that challenges both their and our expectations, and counters the brightly-colored, sugary animated fare we've become accustomed to. As a writer, I tried to embrace it. It's a story full of fun action and adventure and the occasional pratfall, but it's also an opportunity to teach some of the most unpleasant truths kids eventually learn, and reinforce those ideas for us adults who might've forgotten or chose to ignore them.

JS: It is great you were able to delve into this and still pursue your passions for games and comics. As a writer, do you see your role as different on comics, games, and film? Do you find it distracting to work in all three?

AW: Not really. I'm always just trying to tell the best story I can. I feel like working in one medium helps me write better in others. Comics might be the most difficult, only because your space is so limited. I'm always blown away by writers and artists who can create a brand-new compelling world in twenty pages. An action sequence that might take a minute in a movie or game might take four or five pages in a comic, so you're forced to be more economical with your storytelling, and fight the urge to use narration and captions as the sole use of building your characters and your world. It's a fun challenge, and with comics, games, TV, and movies, you're always depending on a lot of other people to tell the story you have in your head. I've been really fortunate to work with a bunch of amazing artists who always surpass my expectations, and make me look way better than I actually am.

JS: Thank you, Allen. This has been a great interview and I am sure many of my writers will be inspired by the work you have done and especially *The Tale of the Seas*. What is next on the table for you?

AW: I'm writing three unannounced projects I'm really excited about, including an upcoming comic series for BOOM! Studios.

Interview: Tomiko Breland, Publisher and Editor

I am happy to share my interview with Tomiko Breland, who I had the pleasure of meeting at my time in the JHU MA in writing program. Tomiko is a fiction writer and an Associate Publisher at The Zharmae Publishing Press. She won the Ploughshares Emerging Writer's Contest and is working on a novel. Additionally, she has an editing/graphic design freelance business, called Paper Star Editorial & Design (www.paperstareditorial.com).

***

Justin Sloan: Tomiko, thank you so much for agreeing to this interview. I am sure my readers would love to hear your thoughts on what it means to be a freelancer and how one goes about finding projects. The site looks amazing, by the way.

Tomiko Breland: Thanks! For me, being self-employed and owning a small business means exactly what it sounds like: It means having the freedom to turn away work, to work from wherever I happen to be, and to spend my day with my son at the park instead of in front of my computer if the whim strikes me. In reality, though, it also means *never* turning away work, and often passing on days at the park because you can't miss a deadline. Finding projects is a matter of putting yourself out there and making connections; you absolutely need to have a professional website and business cards—even if you only get one bite for every 500 hits on your site or 100 cards you hand out, that's something. And you can't forget about old connections, either; think back to anyone or any company you used to have a connection to that might have need for a freelancer now. Lots of companies are scaling back on full-time employees these days and sending their writing, editing, or graphic design projects out-of-house.

JS: Do you believe an education, such as the JHU MA in writing, is necessary to be taken seriously as a freelancer? What would you say to writers who are considering writing programs?

TB: People will take you seriously as a freelancer when you have experience, and when you have a legitimate, recognizable client list. If you're just starting out and you have neither of those, then having a solid degree in your back pocket just may be the factor that sets you apart from other candidates and gets your foot in the door. And it's more than just a credential; there's a reason writing programs like the Johns Hopkins MA exist—they exist to make good writers better. One con to attending a writing program is that some programs are rumored to churn out writers who are carbon copies of one another, or who parrot a particular style. Another is the cost, which can be prohibitive if you haven't yet gotten a good foothold in the freelance business. The pros, however, outweigh the cons—as I find they tend to do when you're talking about education. You'll become a better writer, you'll find your voice (even if you think you already have it), and you'll make connections that may sustain your writing career well into the future.

JS: Working in publishing is a dream of many aspiring writers out there. Where should one look to find positions in the industry? Is it about the network, or do you go to certain sites for these positions?

TB: Networking is important, but I'm sure I have little to say about making connections that others haven't already said, and said well. My suggestion is to look to the boring (i.e., unglamorous) places first: nonprofits, government agencies, tech companies. Get some work under your belt writing marketing material, technical manuals, even tax code (which was my first gig right after undergrad!). Then work your way up the glamour scale: Move on to websites (Demand Media

Studios is a great place to start—they're always looking for people to write and edit short web articles); print publications for small, local newspapers and magazines; and then, once you've got a few good clippings, target the bigger, national publications. If all else fails, contact some nonprofits and charities and offer to write for their newsletter, brochure, or website pro bono—they may take you up on it, and you'll get a good piece to add to your portfolio. If you're looking to apply for writing gigs, you can't beat MediaBistro; and Writer's Market is great, too, though you have to pay for access to their resources. If you're interested in other parts of publishing outside of writing (editorial, for example), you've usually got to start at the ground level—as an editorial assistant or an intern.

JS: Thank you so much for the advice on freelancing—it may seem like common sense to you, but to many aspiring writers out there, it is a whole new world. Stepping back to the world of publishing, can you tell us more about Zharmae publishing? What should aspiring authors consider when submitting their novels? Are there any projects you are especially excited about at the moment?

TB: Zharmae is a quickly-growing company with a fantastic staff who are totally dedicated to putting out awesome reading. In 2013 we published just 10 books, and in 2014 we're up to 63. In 2015, we have 120 books on the publication slate! We lean toward the more spec-fic end of the spectrum, but we also have imprints that publish nonfiction, memoir, action/adventure, middle grade, young adult, new adult, and literary fiction. One thing that sets us apart from other publishers is that we are really willing to work with first-time authors; in fact, most of the authors we sign are new to publishing. My advice to aspiring authors is the same I would give to anyone looking to submit anywhere: Read the submission guidelines, and make sure you stick to them. And then be patient. We get hundreds upon hundreds of submissions, and we take a great deal of care reviewing each one—and that takes time. Also, make sure your story is as good as you can make it before you submit: you've revised it, had others read it, edited it...you shouldn't submit until you're at the point where you feel like every change you make could simply be making it worse!

I'm really excited about a lot of upcoming books, but especially *Romeo and Juliet vs. Zombies* (by Koji Sakai), which is a totally fun read and really well written; and *The Chronicles of Ara: Creation* (by Joel Eisenberg and Steven Hillard), which is the first in a series about the origins of creation—it's the reverse-engineered myth of the muse told through stories about some of the greatest authors of sci-fi and fantasy. The eight-book saga has already been picked up for a television series! And then there's also *Whole in the Clouds*, which is a middle-grade title (available for presale right now!) about a misfit girl who travels to a magical world; it reminds me a bit of my childhood favorites, like *A Wrinkle in Time*.

JS: What about once an author is published, what have you seen authors do that really helps them get their work out there?

TB: There's a reason that agents and publishers nowadays are looking for writers who already have a platform—it helps! If you can build a readership or a following now (via blog, social media, etc.), before you get published, it's reasonable to assume that those readers or followers will buy your book once it's published. Or at least know it exists, and think about buying it—which is already a step in the right direction. So think about creating a blog or providing some other useful or interesting content that will attract followers. It's especially good if the content you're providing is somehow related to the book(s) you plan to publish.

JS: Winning the Ploughshares Emerging Writer's Contest is a great accomplishment. Congrats! Can you share with

us more information about this particular short story and its journey?

TB: Thank you! I'm really honored and humbled. This particular story, I wrote while I was in school. I wondered how to most effectively and efficiently tell the past, present, and future within a short story without the traditional use of flashbacks. With novels, you obviously have the advantage of space, but not with a short story. This story, called "Rosalee Carrasco," resulted. It was extremely challenging to write, but I find that the most challenging stories are often the most rewarding—and it went down on paper the first time in more or less its final draft, so that was fortunate, too. As for submitting to contests, it can be a little more difficult, because there is often a guest editor, and, even if you're familiar with the kinds of stories a journal publishes, you might not be familiar with that particular guest editor's tastes. But there's no reason not to try! Your story just may be the one that resonates with an editor, even if that same journal rejected it in the past. And winning a contest is a great achievement to put on your cover letter in the future.

JS: That is really wonderful. Before we sign off, do you have any last words of advice for other aspiring writers, or any updates on upcoming projects of yours?

TB: "You miss 100% of the shots you don't take." Wayne Gretzky said this, but it's applicable in all aspects of life, not least in writing. Submit, submit, submit. If you don't have the stomach for rejection, you don't have the backbone for writing. The story I won the Ploughshares Emerging Writer's Contest for was rejected 12 times by other journals over 2 years. Publishing is subjective; just because one (or 12 or 50) editors don't choose your work, it doesn't mean the work isn't worthy. Just keep trying.

Interview: Bruce Spiegelman, Starting with Indie Films

Through a screenwriting class taught at The Writer's Salon in Berkeley, I had the pleasure to meet Bruce Spiegelman. Bruce is a longtime contributor on DoneDealPro, though I will not reveal his username here, and his posts show that he knows what he is talking about. He also has co-written three feature films (*Coming Home for Christmas, The Wedding Chapel, and The Bouquet*). Bruce was kind enough to share his thoughts on writing, contests, conferences, screenwriting books, and the industry.

***

Justin Sloan: It is great to have met you in Terrel Seltzer's class, Bruce. Thank you for agreeing to the interview. What brought you to this screenwriting class?

Bruce Spiegelman: I needed a jump-start. My writing partner and I had completed three films in a very short period of time. All were low budget (less than 1.5 million) "faith and family friendly" films, and one of the things you learn with low budget, is that the companies that produce these do them fast. Start to finish is less than a year generally, and in the case of one of them it was less than seven months.

The last film we wrote together was a Christmas film and it wasn't exactly a joyful and triumphant experience. The pressure left some scars between my writing partner and myself, so I decided to take a few months off. A few months became six months during which I was flirting with a different project every week. I wasn't committing to anything and I realized I needed to get back on track. The best way to do that, for me, is to be accountable to something or someone. So I decided I'd take a class and commit to one script till the end using

33

what was being taught each week.

JS: I am glad you are back at it! I agree that a class, and surrounding ourselves with other writers, are great ways to get the writing mojo flowing. Do you have a grand scheme planned out for your screenwriting career, or do you see it as more of a side gig?

BS: It's definitely not a side gig and I certainly have goals, but to plot out a grand scheme in this business is difficult. Too many variables to plot out a single road and hope to only stay on that path.

For instance, I had never planned on writing "faith and family friendly" films. Those types of movies aren't of real interest to me and they really aren't in my wheelhouse, but the opportunity fell into my lap so I wrote the first one...and then was asked to write another one.

I believe that if you want to achieve any kind of success in this business you must set goals and strive to reach them, but you cannot put blinders on and only take the opportunities that you first dreamed of. We all have passion projects that we daydream about, but if you really want to do them you have to prove you can make someone else money with a bunch of stuff that sells first.

JS: What would be your advice to screenwriters trying to get a movie made? How did you go about selling the scripts that you have sold, and would you say this is still a viable way to go about it?

BS: It's really very simple. Explore every avenue and "collect" people while doing it. If there's one great truth in screenwriting I've learned it's this: There are a lot of fantastic writers that will never have a script read by a decision-maker and there are a lot of mediocre writers that will enjoy the thrill of watching their name scroll by during the credits. Writing is only one side of this business. The other side is...business. Spend as much time on the business side of things as you do on writing. Get involved everywhere you can whether it be in contests, film festivals, online communities like Triggerstreet and DoneDealPro, writing groups, etc. Very few specs sell from new writers, but it's possible to get hired for a job when someone in your "network" recommends you. Other writers and producers remember you if you've contributed to their early successes and it will almost always lead to a door being opened.

Most writers believe they can write a good script and someone's going to knock on their door. It's not going to happen that way. A million guys (and girls) write scripts. That's the easiest part of the job. The hard part is the business and networking side.

JS: As for story, what draws you to a story, and keeps you there until the end?

BS: I don't think there's any one thing. There are times I go along for the ride because I'm fascinated by a great character. Another time it may be because I'm learning something new about an era, a lifestyle or an event I haven't been exposed too before. Sometimes it's just a great plot. But we've all watched some awful movies and read some awful stories that we stayed with because we want to know what happens. So I guess in the end it's an emotional involvement that's most important. Curiosity, empathy, love, hate, a hope for justice.

JS: Have you used any script consultants, and are there any you highly recommend? Would you say there is a value of using script consultants above workshops?

BS: Yes to the second question but with a caveat—do your research. A lot of consultants are a waste of money. A few—the real professionals—are worth far more than you pay them.

Most working writers network with other working writers and have a built in network of "consultants" to give them notes. Most also have managers that can perform that function. At some point, in my opinion, every new writer needs a go-to group of professionals to give his or her script a fresh look and it needs to be a professional.

I often send a treatment or very rough first draft to a consultant and then send it again after an extensive rewrite. After the next rewrite I'll usually get a second opinion from another consultant. I know that a lot of writers believe that spending money on your scripts is a waste of time, and I've never understood this. I can't think of another discipline or career where people bat an eyebrow at spending money to learn. Buying books, taking classes, using consultants are the norm in almost every industry, but for some reason writers don't think it's necessary.

As to personal recommendations:

(1) Andrew Hilton (The Screenplay Mechanic) – I will never send out a script without getting notes from him. Ever.

(2) Scott Mullen – The bargain of the century.

(3) Script Gal – Busy. But worth the wait.

JS: Thank you for the recommendations. I have received notes from The Screenplay Mechanic as well, and can vouch for his valuable feedback. You mentioned contests, and I have seen your name pop up under some screenplay contests out there. Are you still submitting to screenplay contests, and what is your advice to aspiring screenwriters regarding such contests?

BS: Use every avenue to get your writing noticed. The good contests can help with that and really aren't that expensive. I can't submit to some of them anymore but I'd still submit a spec to the good ones that I'm eligible for. My opinion on the good ones: Nicholl, Austin, and TrackingB.

JS: I understand you owned Legends Comics and Cards. Can you tell us more about the experience of owning a comic store?

BS: My partner and I owned five comic and card stores in Texas and Louisiana for a number of years. We consulted for Sotheby's, travelled extensively buying collections, met and became life-long friends with many legendary writers and artists. During those years we bought and sold pretty much every major key issue in existence. And I loved every minute doing those things. As you can imagine, the day-to-day grind of running multiple retail locations was not always quite as fun.

The ironic thing about those years is I never once considered becoming a writer. I spent hundreds of hours with great writers and it never crossed my mind.

JS: Do you find your love of comics has helped in your screenwriting?

BS: Comics are a visual story-telling medium, just like films. We have all learned about screenwriting prior to typing out our first "Fade-in." We've absorbed it from films we've seen, stories we've heard, and—for a lot of us—the comics we've read. I believe that in many respects I'm an average writer, but an above average storyteller; and much of that came from spending tens of thousands of hours reading while growing up. Comics were certainly a part of that.

JS: I also understand you studied psychology and marketing. Both of those seem like they would tie directly into screenwriting, with psychology helping to make interesting character, and marketing to help on the business side of selling a script. Has this been in your thought process as you approach screenwriting, from an artistic and business point of view?

BS: My business background is the only reason I've ever sold a script, in my opinion. One more time: selling a script or getting a writing job hinges as much on your ability to market yourself as anything else.

I don't think my initial foray into psychology helped much. I started with that as a major because there were some really hot women at Michigan State (and then LSU) studying psychology in the 1980s. Unfortunately, once they realized I collected comics that plan [to meet women] crashed, and I decided to change majors.

JS: As we close out our interview, do you have any last-minute advice or recommended resources you would like to share with aspiring screenwriters?

BS: Read books. If you get only great idea or learn one important thing from every book you buy it's well worth the $15.00. One great idea can help sell a million dollar script.

Read scripts. There are thousands available for free. Read one a day or one a week—just do it religiously and on a schedule and you'll get better with every one.

Write scripts. Not half a script. Not a few scenes. Finish them. Most will suck but it's the best way to learn.

Put together a network. Participate everywhere you can with people in the industry or trying to get in. Read scripts from other new writers and send them notes. Join a writing group or two—they can be an intense but fantastic way to learn (if you have a thick skin.)

Write every day. No excuse.

PART TWO: LEARNING TO WRITE

When you are starting to learn to write, consider the multitude of paths available. Consider writing groups and the multitude of books on writing. Read the interviews in this book for advice on writing and writing programs. There are many blogs and articles listing top programs in fiction (like the Iowa Writers Workshop and JHU) and screenwriting (American Film Institute, University of Southern California, New York University, University of California, Los Angeles, etc.). I will spend time in this section on the programs I know about, as well as discussing related programs on a macro level.

Since many of my readers may have full-time careers, I will focus less on the full-time writing programs. That said, if quitting your job and going to the Iowa Workshop for literary fiction or to University of Southern California (USC) for film school is your thing, I think it would be a great path. I have discussed such programs briefly below, as have interviewees such as Jeremy Breslau. Make sure to do your research so you know what sort of gamble you are taking. Regardless of what medium of creative writing you are hoping to get into, the pages that follow should be useful.

Choose Your Writing Program

I am addicted to education, almost as much as I am addicted to writing. But there comes a point when we must all ask ourselves where our priorities lie and decide how much time to spend learning versus actually writing.

With that disclaimer out of the way, I would like to promote the idea of furthering your writing education. Too often I see people who say they want to be writers but have not bothered to study the craft. Being well read is certainly important, but you need to know what editors, agents, managers, and other gatekeepers are looking for nowadays. You need to understand what omniscient is versus third person or first person in fiction, and that, while authors such as Charles Dickens and Victor Hugo were great, their style of writing is a harder sell today. This greater understanding of modern fiction and the market is one advantage of taking classes. Likewise, you need to understand why choices are made in screenwriting, because screenplays that sell often incorporate unusual formatting and you do not want be to all over the place trying to understand which one is right or why one style is being used. The same is true with video games, in that you will probably never truly understand how important player ownership and agency is in every scene of a game simply by playing games. This is all information you may be able to learn from a great mentor in the industry, but until you have one, obtaining an education may be for you.

Another, and probably more important, reason to enroll in such programs is to see what sorts of mistakes other novice writers are making. If you have never workshopped your material and provided feedback to others, this experience is a must. Too often we have blinders on and are unable to see our own faults; but once you see that writer Billy Bob constantly uses the word "just" and never uses any of the five senses aside from sight, you may start to see similar issues in your own writing. Additionally, it is important to have an instructor or someone more experienced than the rest of the group moderating, to avoid groupthink and everyone leaning toward an amateur way of thinking.

I have taken a variety of classes and been a member of several critique groups. Among those, pursuing an MA in writing at JHU was one of my best experiences. As a point of reference, the program is two years in length. It includes classes on modern American authors, the power of the sentence, advanced revision techniques, and even the occasional classes on screenwriting or young adult fiction. All classes take place on nights and weekends, which was perfect for me since I was working full-time. This also means a lot of your colleagues will have jobs, and therefore other life experiences that they will be able to write about.

While attending JHU, I met many friends who shared my passion for writing (see interviews with Tomiko Brelend and Kelly Ann Jacobson). I received very valuable feedback from instructors and students, and was able to work one-on-one with a professor on my novel. Attending JHU gave me the opportunity to intern for *The Doctor T.J. Eckleburg Review*. If you are serious about writing, how could you not want such an experience? Research the many great MFA and MA in writing programs out there.

If you cannot afford such a program (ranging from $20,000 to $50,000 for two to three years), attend local writing classes or writing groups. If time is your issue, consider low-residency programs. I hear Spalding has a great one. My thought is that you are going to be writing anyway, so it is not really extra work to attend such a program. Think of it as focused work.

Some writers need to write and desire to be writing at all times, while others want to write but must force themselves. If you fall into this first category, you are going to write no matter how much time you spend in classes or working on blogs, because you love to write. If you fall into the second category, you still may make it, but you need to focus. You may want a program to structure you, or you may be the type who should take one or two classes to learn what you can, but then focus your time on actually writing. I do not comprehend the second category of writers, but I imagine that you will eventually find yourself loving what you are doing and will fall into the first category, or you will give up. However, I have read interviews of professional writers who say they hate to write, and they are doing just fine (Jonathan Nolan of *Interstellar* and *The Dark Knight,* among other amazing films, is one of them).[3] Whether you like writing or not, find the system that works best for you and get your words on the page.

For helpful thoughts on attending USC's MFA program, see my interview with Jeremy Breslau. He makes the point that what you learn in film school ensures the work you are putting into the world is of a professional quality, and that the networking experience is invaluable. USC is a great school, among great company, and if you are able to attend, you probably should give it some major consideration.

For those of you interested in screenwriting for film or video games, it is worth discussing the UCLA certificate program. Before enrolling in the UCLA School of Theater, Film, and Television's Professional Program in Screenwriting, I had my misgivings. For one, I live outside of LA and couldn't comprehend

---

[3] Jonathan Nolan's IMDB Page, http://www.imdb.com/name/nm0634300/

how an online class could be worth the cost. You receive a certificate, but what good is a certificate? However, I soon started meeting writers whose writing I greatly admire and who had attended this program. They could not speak highly enough about it, and now neither can I.

Having only done the online class, I will focus on that aspect of the program. Online classes meet once a week for three hours on Skype. In my case, our class met every Wednesday from 6:00 to 9:00 p.m., with short breaks between classes. The first class focused on completing a spec episode (an episode of a current show on television), and in the next two classes we completed one pilot (or original concept) per 10 week class. Although the classes were organized as workshops, the teachers still made plenty of time for instruction and were available for discussion outside of class.

The price of the online programs was, at the time of writing this, $3,500 for the year. I used to have an issue with paying for classes like this, because it is so easy to start your own workshop and get people together via MeetUp.com. However, the instruction in this program is stellar, and the fact that everyone has paid means you get some serious writers as classmates who will make sure to pump out pages for your workshops. That atmosphere of dedication justifies the tuition.

The UCLA program offers professional certificates in features, television sitcoms, television drama, and video game writing. That last one sounds especially interesting to me, as I am a video game writer. Furthermore, in the first iteration of the video game writing class, the instructors were the writers behind *God of War,* an amazing series of games. If you are able to pursue the video game writing certificate, please reach out to me and let me know what you think. Maybe a guest blog will be in order? The other programs speak for themselves, and I have heard great things about all of them.

The UCLA professional program has some amazing instructors, many of whom work on current shows and are very approachable, intelligent, and encouraging. They have made me rethink how I approach outlining, given me a better understanding of character development, and helped me to understand the structure of television writing and why it is done a certain way. If you want instructors who will inspire you to push your writing craft to the next level, I highly recommend looking up the UCLA professional program, either in person or online.

I should say that the UCLA program is not paying me in any way for promoting their program. The purpose of including it here is to share yet another way to improve your writing, wherever you may live. If you are working full-time, UCLA's program can fit into your schedule and not break your bank. If you have questions about the program, feel free to reach out to me. If you are already sold on the program, good luck and have fun!

Join a Writing Group

Especially when you are starting out, I would advise you make sure to find a writing group. Before I had children, I made a point of attending writing conferences and film festivals. I made a short film and I set up meetings with folks at Disney, Pixar, Electronic Arts, and DreamWorks, among others. All this networking reminded me of the importance of having a writing group, because at the end of the day it really is all about having a superb writing sample. Very few of us are able to create a great story in a vacuum. Like Shane Black says, when you get to Hollywood you want to have three great scripts in your pocket. Likewise, you want to write multiple books, not spend your whole life on that first one. Sit down and write-write-write, and then workshop and rewrite-rewrite-rewrite.

For a while I led a screenwriting group in the East Bay, was a member of a fiction writers group in San Francisco, and was a member of various online critique groups. I found having all these writing groups necessary. That said, be sure to find the writing group (or groups) that works for you. The best ones are those with a variety of skill levels. If you are all complete beginners, your workshop may lead to groupthink and rigid or unhelpful advice.

Writing is subjective, and the main lesson I take away from the pros at the Austin Film Festival or the San Francisco Writers Conference is that we each have our own system of writing. The rules are B.S. It is best if you can find a writing group with some actual filmmakers or published authors. However, if you are only able to find a group of novices, do not worry. We all have to start somewhere. These fellow novices in your workshop are the folks who will be most likely to bring you up with them, or who may be interested in starting a writing partnership with you. An example is Shane Black's roommate situation when he was starting out; another is the Inklings, where J.R.R. Tolkien and C.S. Lewis, among others, got their starts. As Brandon Sanderson says in his "Writing Excuses" podcast, it was not a coincidence that so many in the Inklings group were successful.

The level of your writing group's success also depends on how active your writing group is. You should be meeting fairly often, and maybe have other activities aside from simply critiquing. My fiction group had holiday parties and got together whenever one of our members published a book. This habit of meeting outside of critiques encourages the level of trust and friendship necessary for a strong critique group; and if you are involved in these activities you show that you are there to be part of the group, not just to show up from time to time to get help on your story.

More import than who is in your group or how often you meet is how active you are when you meet. You cannot simply attend and say "I agree" to everything. Put some real energy into your feedback (which is easier, in my opinion, if you get to see the work before the meeting).

If you are trying to find a writing group, see MeetUp.com for groups that meet up for all sorts of causes, from running to film-watching. You can attend a writer's conference or film festival and ask around; maybe even talk to the panelists (if they are local) and see if they know of any groups. Doing exactly this at the San Francisco Writers Conference is how I found one of my writing groups.

If none of these methods for finding a writing group work for you, start your own group. You can use MeetUp.com, though it costs a small monthly fee. To cover that fee, my group would collect a donation of $1 per member per meeting. You can always try craigslist to find members as well. I recommend you request writing samples before accepting members, to at least make sure your members have a basic understanding of the writing craft.

You can structure the group however you want, but here is how my writing groups conducted our critique sessions:

1. Screenwriters: Members sent out up to 30 pages of their screenplay before we would meet, then bring five to seven pages of their script to hear how it sounded when read aloud. We assigned roles from the script to each group member, including one reader as the narrator, and everyone would read the script while its writer listened and stayed quiet. Then we went around the table, critiquing the full 30 pages and whatever might have come up while we were listening to the five to seven pages. We gave first our positive comments and then our constructive criticism. We played around with other methods, but this seemed to work the best for us and it allowed four to five people a turn to get their work critiqued in a two-hour window.

2. Fiction Writers: We sent around up to 10 pages a week before the meeting, and then expected everyone to come ready to discuss the pages. We took turns focusing on each person's writing, saying first what worked for us, and then what we felt needed help.

When looking for locations for a writing group, I recommend checking your local library to see if they have private rooms. Unfortunately, some libraries' private rooms (such as the ones that would have been convenient for the members of my writing group) require booking well in advance. Coffee shops work, but make sure there is plenty of space and the coffee shop is not too loud. Restaurants can work, but speak with the manager first and make sure they are fine with you all taking up two hours of their seating space. Also, encourage all of your members to order food, or at least a drink, if you go to a cafe or restaurant.

In addition to making an effort to attend your critique meetings and provide insightful critiques, consider other ways you can help your writing group get ahead. Start a website for your group, or a group blog, which was how my blog BayAreaScreenwriters.com came into being. Attend other events and share what you have learned at those events with your group; or, even better, get them to go with you to these events. If you hear about an opportunity, pass it on. And when you strike it big, grab your group members by the lapels and pull them up with you. I know that my writing groups were full of members who will help each other however and whenever possible.

Develop Your Characters

Learning to create three-dimensional characters is, for me, at the top of the priority list for writing prose, screenplays, or video games. Whether you are looking at the next Tyrion Lannister (*Game of Thrones*, or *A Song of Ice and Fire*), or Billy Lynch (*Charming Billy*), you are seeing a well thought-out character that an author spent many hours contemplating. If you want your fiction to shine anywhere near the level of such authors as George R.R. Martin or Alice McDermott, you must spend the requisite time getting to know your characters.

Do you have to write a character bio for each of your characters? Not necessarily. But if you like to explore while you write, I recommend you at least keep track of everything you discover in these creative explorations, so you can later reference this record as well as check it for inconsistencies. Trust me, it is hard to keep all of that information in your head. In one of my UCLA writing classes we were told to write "Character X is a character who...." and fill in the blank. Simple yet satisfying. For example, "Tyrion Lannister is a character who seeks acceptance through the use of gold and through his quest for knowledge often found in books." That is my interpretation of Tyrion, at any rate. You can put other things about Tyrion there, like the fact that he enjoys whores, but for me this description explains what truly makes Tyrion who he is and causes him to act how he does at every moment.

Do not forget to look at your character on a macro level, as well as a micro and per chapter level. Really consider what your characters' motivations are in each chapter, what their goals and expectations are, how they fail (or succeed) in their attempts, and how they make us fall in love with them (if that is the goal). Think about how the characters feel about each other, and how their actions may change these dynamics. The common saying is that they do not have to be likable, just

49

interesting. If you are going the anti-hero route, as in Breaking Bad, what are you doing to make that character three-dimensional so that we can at least relate on some level? Breaking Bad was an excellent example, because the protagonist got involved in the drug game when he found out he had cancer and not long to live but needed money to care for his family, a family that included a son with a disability.

If you want to really get into the details, and I certainly recommend doing this at least once, try one technique that I learned at JHU. My professor had me set up an overall timeline for the novel, saying who did what, when they did it, and what those actions meant for each character, emotionally. Next I had to set up a timeline for my main characters, from birth to the end of the book, with main events in their lives and, once again, how each moment affected my characters emotionally. This was an amazing experience and I learned so much about my characters. Best of all, my novel improved considerably when I looked at it with this level of detail.

To develop your characters is simple advice, but so often I see people writing a short story, book, or screenplay without putting in the time to know their characters. If you do not care enough about your characters to get to know them, then neither will your readers.

Part Two Next Steps

This is where I will task you with looking deep within and asking: Is my writing the best it can be? The answer is never yes, not if you are a real writer, because we can always improve. Therefore, I want you to put together a plan for improving your craft. Look up local classes or writing groups, or find some online classes or critique groups. Watch movies, read books and screenplays, and play some games. Include these methods of improvement on your goal list that sits next to your computer, and get to it. Imagine your favorite filmmaker or novelist or video game company just asked to read your material—now think of this moment as one year in the future, but you know it is coming. How can you reach a level where you will not be hesitant to pass your work on to the professionals? Make it happen.

My Learning Plan

1. What classes can I take over the next year? Over the next five years?

2. What writing groups or organizations can I join in the next year? In the next five years?

3. What conferences can I attend in the next year? In the next five years?

4. How many books and screenplays can I read, movies can I watch, or video games can I play—and which ones—over the next year? Over the next five years?

Interview: Will Wight, Author of the *Traveler's Gate* Trilogy

You know when you read a novel and you cannot put it down? How awesome is it when that same book turns out to be part of a trilogy? And you get to spend three books with these amazing characters battling through crazy territories with fire and ice and crazy swords and a guy who talks to dolls? If this is not making sense to you, then you probably have not read Will Wight's Traveler's Gate trilogy. If this is so, stop reading this and go get *House of Blades*, the first book in the trilogy. When you are done with the trilogy, join me in hearing what Will Wight had to say about writing.

I have included Will's interview at the end of Part Two because he is a perfect example of how spending time on learning the craft can result in a self-driven success. He went straight into an MFA program from undergrad, published the first book of his trilogy, and has had some success working as an author. The result of his drive to write was that he did not have to find a mediocre desk job like many of us have to do in order to pay the bills—he is a writer who pays his bills through his writing. We have much to learn from Will.

***

Justin Sloan: Will, thank you so much for agreeing to speak with me. As you know, I love your books and your writing style. Can you tell us a little bit about your background and how you came up with this amazing idea for a trilogy?

Will Wight: For me, the ideas have always been the easy part. I collect bits and pieces of a story from everywhere: song lyrics, bumper stickers, desktop wallpapers, Reddit. The trick is sifting through all those little pieces and putting them together in a way that makes sense.

In terms of *House of Blades* specifically, I had several different core ideas for the plot, world, magic system, and characters. The magic system came from a little fantasy I've had for years: sometimes, I just want to step into my own little world where no one can get to me. In the universe of the Traveler's Gate trilogy, that's a superpower. The essential idea for the plot came from a frustration I've always had with fantasy novels. Namely, that the hero who miraculously inherits all of his power is usually a pretentious, self-focused jerk.

I wouldn't like that guy in real life, so I decided to tell the story from a slightly different perspective.

JS: And you pulled it off exceptionally. When it comes to writing, do you have a method to the madness?

WW: No, it's mostly just madness. I had a one-page brief outline of the plot before I started writing, and then as I got to know the world and the magic system a little more, I expanded the outline. Then I just kind of sat down and let words come out. Over and over.

JS: That sounds similar to my process, though I often have to go back and update the outline to make sure I'm not going off on a crazy path. How much do you think that your writing education played into your ability to pull off such awesome writing? For other authors looking to mimic your success, would you say a degree in creative writing or an MFA is a necessity?

WW: For me, it was a necessity. But for you? No, you'll be fine. I learned a great deal over the course of my Master's degree in Creative Writing, but it's nothing you can't learn on your own.

That said, there's no way I would have learned it on my own. I just don't have the kind of self-discipline it would take to find a mentor, join a writing group, and read a bunch of books on the writing craft. I needed the MFA coursework because it gave me the structure that forced me to do all that.

The classes teach you to look at writing as a skill that takes time, effort, and training. Without that perspective, you won't be able to write at a professional level. If you already know that and you're willing to put in the work, then you're ready to start.

JS: In our previous discussions, you mentioned the importance of finding a good editor, making a great cover, and writing multiple books. Do you have any thoughts on how one should find people to edit or do book design? I know the San Francisco Writers Conference introduces writers to editors, but what would you recommend we look for in an editor? How about with an artist for the cover?

WW: You can find great editors or graphic designers with a couple of hours online. There are even some professional book covers you can get on sale for cheap. But there's one keyword in there that you shouldn't overlook: professional. If you want your book to stand out, then it needs to look professional.

Don't publish your book without getting someone to edit it first. Someone who knows what they're doing; not your mom. And I beg you, don't draw your own cover. If you're not a graphic artist who actually makes a living producing art for other people, you're not qualified to draw a book cover. Beg, borrow, or steal the money it takes to buy a real artist's time. I promise you, you will make that money back.

JS: That's a big promise, but I hope it's true. On the topic of writing multiple books, I imagine a series or trilogy is the best, but what do you think about the idea of writing books in other genres? Will Amazon still help market your other books if one is fantasy and one is literary or mystery?

WW: Now, why would I want to write a book that isn't fantasy? Magic makes everything better! From firsthand experience, I know that releasing a new book is the best advertisement for your old books. Based on what I've heard from other writers, this works even cross-series and cross-genre.

But take that with a hefty crystal of salt, because I've never written outside the fantasy genre myself. Seriously, why would I?

JS: Are there any books on writing out there that you would recommend?

WW: There are so many great books on writing that it's difficult to narrow it down. Jim Butcher's Livejournal was a great help to me, even though it's not strictly a book; and I'm a huge fan of Stephen King's *On Writing*. But there's an abundance of excellent material out there teaching you the craft.

I'd say that many aspiring writers think they need to find the hidden treasure trove of writing secrets before they can write a book that people will read. Really, they just need to seize the information that's already out there, freely available. Then they need to hone their skills, which you can only do by shutting up, sitting down, and writing.

JS: Thank you, Will. Before we sign off, can you tell us what you have coming up? I know everyone is looking forward to the next trilogy by Will Wight!

WW: My next work is entitled *Of Sea and Shadow*, and I'm hoping to have it out this coming winter. It's set in a world entirely separate from the *Traveler's Gate* trilogy, and it's got Lovecraftian elder gods, pirates, assassins, muskets, enchanted swords, and a global empire that's slowly falling apart. I've been having a lot of fun with it. After that, I don't know. I'll probably wander the earth as a lonely samurai, writing wrongs and folding paper into cranes.

Interview: Jeremy Breslau, Writer and Director of *1982*

I find myself surrounded by extremely talented individual in the video game world. Allow me to introduce Jeremy Breslau, a fellow writer at Telltale Games as well as a filmmaker (writer and director) and USC alum. Be sure to watch his short film *1982*, which will be discussed in this interview. I included Jeremy's interview under this section because he went to film school and has worked in Hollywood and now video games. He is a screenwriter and director, and when you watch his work you will discern the true level of professionalism with which he approaches his projects.

***

Justin Sloan: Thank you for taking time out of your busy schedule to help me and my readers. You are unique among my interviewees in that you recently moved from LA to the Bay Area. What inspired this move, and do you feel you will be hindered at all as a filmmaker by the fact that you live outside of LA?

Jeremy Breslau: Hi Justin. Thanks for chatting with me. As much as I love LA, I was there for 14 years, and I was inspired to move because I wanted to live in a more beautiful setting that I thought would be a better place for my son to spend his early years. I've always loved the San Francisco and Marin area, and when the opportunity to move came up, my wife and I thought it was the right time for a change. In terms of my filmmaking, I was fortunate that during the course of my projects in LA I built a wonderful team and network of supporters, and I don't need to be in LA 24/7 to work with them. I also find the change of scenery to be inspiring.

JS: I am happy to hear it and I could not agree more—the

scenery in Northern California is inspiring. What about the video game industry attracted you? Do you think there's a big difference between writing for film and writing for video games?

JB: I've enjoyed playing video games for as long as I can remember, and I have a strong appreciation for the sophisticated character-centric approach Telltale takes to their games. Although writing for games and films is different in terms of the interactivity a game requires, the reasons an audience (or a player) cares remains the same: nuanced, empathetic characters driving a story worth telling; high stakes, tension, dramatic irony—all the good stuff that makes a narrative compelling.

JS: If you could go back ten or fifteen years and give your younger self advice about the writing, what would it be? Would you follow the same path?

JB: I would follow a similar path, but I would also make sure to heed the advice that a colleague's mentor, Lawrence Kasdan, told him, which seems obvious, but is worth mentioning: write what you love, but make sure it's what an audience can love too (i.e., be sure to know for whom you're writing, and to understand that you're working in a highly competitive business). In other words, you should definitely love what you write, it should come from your heart; but heartfelt and commercial are not mutually exclusive. I always tried to write what I was passionate about and what was commercial, but I think over time I better internalized his message.

JS: Before coming to the video game world, I had considered the USC and have met some great people who went through the program. What would be your advice for others out there applying to the program? Would you recommend it? How can they stand out in their application and prepare themselves for once they are accepted?

JB: I would definitely recommend it. There's a reason it's the number one film school in the world: they teach you the skills to tell a gripping story. It's true that reading screenplays and watching every movie possible will also teach you about the craft, but to have it distilled so clearly and to have to generate material that is then critiqued by peers and professors, all while meeting your future industry connections, is priceless. (Not to mention guest speakers like Steven Spielberg, Robert Zemeckis, and JJ Abrams, to name a few, imparting their personal experiences...) Or their mentor program, where I was lucky enough to be partnered with Oscar-winning screenwriter Steve Zaillian, who graciously took the time to read my screenplays and give me suggestions.

In terms of advice for applying for the program, I think it is great to have as wide a variety of work and life experiences as possible, the more unique the better. Also, be prepared to generate strong and personal writing samples. That, and do not give up. There were many students turned away the first time, only to be accepted when they tried again.

JS: That must have been an amazing experience. Of course, someday I'll be able to say I worked right next to the great Jeremy Breslau, so take that USC. It sounds like you made some amazing contacts, which I hear is often a main reason for attending film school. Do you agree with this and have you seen much help through the alumni network over the years? If someone was a production assistant (PA) already working in the industry but debating film school, what would you advise?

JB: I would say contacts are one very good reason, but not the main reason. I would say the main reason is that film school provides you with a skill set to compete in a hugely competitive industry, where there is zero patience for amateur material. And yes, while it's true that terrible things get made for many reasons, when a reader or prospective representation reads your material, it needs to be gripping—

and, of course, professional. As for the alumni network, I have remained friends with many of my USC peers, who have become vital professional contacts. For these reasons, if someone was a PA working in the industry, and they had the opportunity, I would definitely advise them to go to film school.

JS: Having spoken with you, I know that you have some great experience which helped you meet people and put together an amazing team for your short film *1982*. The website (www.1982short.com) lists the film as follows: "A blocked novelist reflects on a pivotal year in his life, when, as a precocious six-year-old, he struggled for the attention of his bickering parents." For my readers, see the teaser on Vimeo, or the article on Variety411 that largely focuses on Frank Buono and his involvement. The film looks intriguing and the visuals beautiful, and it was great that you were able to work with Mr. Buono, largely known for his work on *Children of Men*. What have you learned from working with such talent?

JB: I was very fortunate to have worked with Frank and the rest of the amazing team. I can also say that when I introduced myself to many of them the fact that I went to USC, and that it was clear that I had professional training and the ambition to make something we could all be proud of, was a major plus (as well as having directed shorts prior for Fox and MTV's Atomfilms). In terms of directing, I've always been a firm believer in planning and rehearsal. But what I learned from Frank was how, if you do your endless prep, and then get tuned into the moment, it frees you to improvise and create beautiful, organic moments on the fly. His cinematography is not only lovely for his mastery of light and mood, but for the suppleness he adds to the movements, which he achieved (from what I witnessed) only by being so tuned into the moment. I can't wait to work with him again—but now that he's an Emerging Cinematographer Award Winner, I might have some competition!

JS: How would you advise young filmmakers to put a crew together? Is it mostly about helping people and hoping they'll help you? What would be some warning signs when talking with folks to see if they belong on your team?

JB: I would advise young filmmakers to surround themselves with the most committed, passionate, knowledgeable peers they can find—preferably who have training in the jobs they're undertaking—and to beg, borrow, and steal to make a short happen. In terms of reaching out to established film professionals: if you have a story worth telling, know how you want to tell it, and are able to raise even a modicum of resources, I would try to find out if you had any personal connections to any of them and use that for an intro. But barring that: reach out, express your appreciation and say that you have a project you want to discuss, and see what happens. You might be surprised—even if the people you first reach out to can't do it, they can sometimes introduce you to someone terrific who can.

JS: How did this experience with *1982* differ from the first short film you wrote and directed?

JB: I directed shorts for Fox and MTV with budgets that they had supplied. For *1982*, my wife, Gina, who produced the film, helped me raise the money. 1982 was also more complex visually than anything I'd ever done before, and required months of prep. As it was such an ambitious project, it was incredibly satisfying to feel that we pulled it off. But that was all due to the extraordinary hard work and commitment of our wonderful crew.

JS: Have you learned one or two main lessons from your experience in short films?

JB: I've learned that if you want to direct features, there's no better way to get your feet wet, and that making a short film is vital to understanding the importance of preparation. It can also be a great testing ground for larger ideas. The bottom line is that the lessons provided by actually going out and making something are invaluable. If you want to make films, you really have to go for it.

JS: Thank you again, Jeremy. I had a great time learning from your answers and loved the short, *1982*. It was touching, disturbing, and beautiful. I can't wait to see what you come up with next! On that note, what do you have in mind? Can we expect a Jeremy Breslau feature in the near future?

JB: We are currently prepping my first feature, *The Chaplain*, a dramatic thriller in the vein of *The Wrestler* and *Winter's Bone*, that I'm proud to say will be made by the same wonderful team behind *1982*.

Interview: Joyce Lee, a View on Women and Writing

Joyce Lee recently sat down with me to discuss screenwriting and the challenges she has faced as an Asian American woman in the world of Hollywood. She created a beautiful and heartfelt animation titled *Paper Words,* featured on PBS, in which "a girl with strong imagination refuses to move from a classroom corner and no one knows why." Additionally Joyce has won awards such as an ABC New Talent Development Grant, the prestigious Women in Film General Motors Emerging Filmmakers Grant, and the Robin Eickman Award. I am happy to say she was willing to share her experience with us. I include her in this section because she has some great experience with various programs available, and writes fiction as well as screenplays. She shares her thoughts with us regarding inspiration, from the perspective of an Asian-American female writer.

***

Justin Sloan: Thank you again for agreeing to this interview, Joyce. I would like to begin by asking if you have one project you are most proud of, and if so, what is it about this project that made you so passionate about it?

Joyce Lee: Thank you so much for inviting me to talk with you. It is an honor to be included.

I can't say that I have any one film or script that I feel more passionate about than another. Any project that I am actively working on, I am very involved with. Otherwise, I can't really sustain the lengthy production process or writing process. I will say that I am proud of *Paper Words,* however. I think it worked well as an animation, and emotionally it seems to engage certain viewers who have undergone some of the issues that the protagonist in the story underwent.

JS: I certainly see that. From your animation Paper Words and your other projects, I see that you write about issues you must care about. Does this story and others you have written about come from a personal place? Where do ideas start for you, and how you do you tackle them?

JL: Inspiration comes from many sources: from events, personal experience, observation, and (believe it or not) dreams. But there was an inciting incident a long time ago that started my habit of making issue-oriented short films. *Foreign Talk,* my first 16mm film came about unexpectedly. I had wanted to make a film that was meaningful but nothing really grabbed me, so I gave myself a deadline of a certain date, about six months into the future. I vowed that if I didn't have an idea by then, I should probably give up doing film.

That day came. I didn't have a really good idea that I felt passionate about and I had an appointment with a friend so I went on the BART train to go meet her. On the way to Fruitvale, I had my life threatened by two men who singled me out for harassment. The timing was synchronistic because I had just finished reading *Angry Women* and felt furious about violence against women. Then I meet these two guys who felt angry about racial inequality and being held down. They were trying to instigate something with me as a way of flexing their power, and I reacted to that. In turn, they got aggressive and threatened to physically injure me, which was terrifying. As they kept their verbal assault going, they would intersperse their angry comments with words about oppression. That triggered an "aha" moment for me. If they were just misogynists, there wouldn't have been anything I could do, but the root of their behavior was driven by the belief that all negative reaction against them was based on racism. Well, that was a subject I could relate to very well. Somehow, I talked my way out of the situation and by the end of the ride, we had a dialogue going, even though I was still on edge and it was all very tense.

That incident sparked my debut film—I suddenly had a topic that I was passionate about. I think that whole experience showed me the importance of producing movies that are personally relevant. I felt such a strong need to share that incident. It helped me feel the difference between ideas that I experimented with versus something I felt passionate about. There is something psychologically cathartic about expressing your feelings in a creative way or calling attention to an issue or a struggle. Deciding how to patch images together is the entertaining part. You shoot a bunch of stuff, edit it together and see if it works or not. Making it into a cohesive story is a process of trial and error. I show my rough cuts to other filmmakers and friends and get feedback, so any film I work on is constantly evolving until I get sick of working on it or it feels like I can't go any further.

Inspiration can come from the strangest places. I read somewhere that Alan Ball was inspired to write *American Beauty* when he saw a plastic bag floating by. I've put dream images in my films, and lately I've relied more on dreams for inspiration. Last week, I had an action adventure dream that was quite filmic, so right now I am tapping in on inner resources more than external events.

JS: Wow, what an experience. I am glad you found the positive from all of that. What are you currently working on, and how do you anticipate putting it out there?

JL: I have been working on a romantic comedy for over a year and a half. I also started two dramatic scripts that I am 30 pages into. I just finished a short story not too long ago. I am experimenting with writing an action comedy and I started a young adult novel. Writing doesn't cost anything but time, so I've been focusing on that for the past few years. I don't know how I am going to get the scripts made. I fall prey to the money-draining scriptwriting contests so many screenwriters outside of the system get sucked into. Not the best route to go, but I had to try it for the experience. I have recently applied to Tribeca All Access to see about getting some seed money to kick off development. For my rom-com, I've figured out a budget of approximately two-million-plus to shoot it right. I have no clue how I am going to get that kind of money. The likely scenario is that I'll just raise a small percentage of that budget and make some major adjustments, such as using unknown talent, having a smaller crew, scaling down the number of locations, and so forth. When I wrote Paper Words, it had started as a feature live-action narrative and was a much different story about a family in turmoil. I had no idea how I was going to get it made. After a while, I realized I had to make some compromises, focus on one character, and turn it into an animation. I don't regret that decision.

JS: You certainly have a lot going on, and you have accomplished so much, with your animation project, feature screenplays, and projects such as *Poetry Inside Out*. Where do you find the time to do so? Do you see them all fitting into one grand plan, or do you approach projects as the inspiration hits you?

JL: It's one of the biggest challenges I have faced over the years, trying to find time to work on things when you have to work a day job to pay bills. I am not a fast writer. It takes me a great deal of time to read aloud what I wrote, to try out dialogue. I also struggle with prose. It doesn't come as naturally to me as it does for someone who grew up speaking solely English at home. I read things over several times in order to choose the right words.

How I managed in the past is that I'd work for a while, then take time off to focus on creative stuff. But nowadays, it's been challenging with this economy. The city I live in has become outrageously expensive. If I have a long-term job that requires more mental commitment and responsibilities, I don't have energy left over to be creative at the end of the day. You might know what that's like, 8 hours on a computer, just to come home to spend two more hours on a computer. That doesn't work for me on a daily basis, so weekends, holidays, days off become the time for writing and planning. It's all slower than I would like. Sometimes, ideas that inspire you get delayed and you lose momentum. Sometimes you can regain that drive and sometimes you can't. If a particular idea doesn't go away, I jot it down whenever I have a spare moment, such as during a commute, or over lunch, but that's certainly not most days. I envy people who can write fast and can write volumes after a stressful day at work.

JS: Do you find there are avenues for those of us outside Los Angeles who want to be screenwriters, or do you think we have to make the move?

JL: It all depends on what your goal is. There are some video post houses and FX facilities here in the Bay Area and some limited production that happens in this city, but most of it is in Southern California or New York. Northern California is for documentary filmmakers and animators. If you want to earn money working in the film industry full-time, you have to move to southern California. Over the years, I've met actors, writers, crew, and film composers who haven't been able to make ends meet working here. They have all moved to LA; and the ones I've kept in touch with seem to be working in the industry, not necessarily working on their own projects, but working for others. It's a lifestyle change to move there, and it's not one that interests me so much. I've been able to make my short films here, but have to do other things to pay the bills and there are long lapses of time between each project. You can get funding if you are making an educational piece, although the competition for those dollars are getting fiercer in this economy, but the moment you want to do a feature-length narrative, Northern California becomes a tough place to be because the money, the producers, the directors, the production companies—the volume just isn't here. The only screenwriter/directors who can do what they like are the few big names we all know. I have struggled with that question too. Screenwriting you can do from anywhere; it's getting the money and right people to see it that's the problem. I think your answer is as good as mine. If you do well in some type of writing competition, or find a producer who likes your work, or have an agent—then you can fly in and make your deals. If you want to write for scripts for a living, then you probably have to be in LA.

JS: Considering all of the awards and recognition you have received, do you have any advice on where to look for such grants and awards? Have you seen them help your career, aside from the monetary value?

JL: I have been fortunate to win some grants and awards that have helped me to start and finish projects. Without them, I wouldn't have been able to make my last two films, so I am eternally grateful for every award and opportunity I've received. The majority of production funding I have received has been for educational film projects. I have also gotten a few grants that were related to narrative projects. Those grants helped improved my understanding of how the whole larger production process works, even if the grants haven't helped in getting a film made. It is all an important learning process and through grants such as the ABC Scholarship Award and the Women in Film General Motors Grant, I've been able to meet people I normally wouldn't have access to.

To get to the level where I could qualify for grants, I had to fund my own projects when I first started out. My film *Foreign Talk* did very well for a short film, and I made other short films after that. Eventually, I developed a small string of films I could say I had produced and directed. My advice to anyone who is applying for grants is that you have to make your first one or two films on your own dime, then publicize like crazy, and get your films screened at as many places as you can.

That will help you qualify for funding. For resources, look to your city and state governments for what is available. There are a number of regional grants that are specific to each area. Also, look for grants that cater to your particular ethnic group if you belong to a minority, or grants that are subject-specific. Consider if your project can go the educational route and tap into CPB money. Create a project that has some cultural, artistic, social, or political relevance in order to attract special interest groups and build a following on social networking sites. Get a fiscal sponsor so that donors can write off their donations to your film project; collaborate with an organization or with a local PBS station; peruse the Foundation Center; join film groups; and do a lot of internet searches for film funding.

For feature narratives, you can try for things like Amazon Studios; approach a production house, and try film markets like IFP. I have heard that a number of online channels now have their own production facilities and/or invest in new projects—including YouTube, but don't quote me on that. I won't lie and say any of this is easy. It's hard. I've been doing this routine a long time and I still haven't made a feature, but I'm trying to do so with this next one. You should also be checking funding possibilities every six months or so, just to see if there are new opportunities that didn't exist before. Through a web search two months ago, I learned about the A3 Asian American Fellowship. It was brand new this year and it wasn't publicized much. Had I not been doing a search for Asian American film funding, I never would have known about it. Just be ready to put some of your own cash and sweat into your projects and don't give up. Develop a thick skin for rejection because you will hear more "no"s than "yes"es. If you keep at it long enough and are flexible about your writing or your film, you'll get the support one way or another—whether you end up funding it yourself or you get investors involved.

JS: What is your advice for young women screenwriters out there? Do you think they face real disadvantages in trying to make it as a screenwriter? Do you have any anecdotes my readers may find useful?

JL: The wonderful thing about being a young female screenwriter is that younger writers are much closer to the pulse of teenage angst and coming-of-age issues than older writers (unless older writers are writing about something from their own past, or another person's story, or about their children). There are certain universal themes we all face—such as the need to be valued, to be loved, to fit in, to have friends, to be heard, to be seen for who we really are—but the details that couch those experiences change from decade to decade. Those changing details lay the groundwork for new stories from younger generations. Young women writers have an opportunity to write about what concerns them most: their hopes, their worries, their most pressing issues. We now live in a time of economic uncertainty that we haven't seen since the Great Depression. Everyone is constantly under a barrage of information overload, and now we're dealing with climate change and loss of resources. Also, social interaction models have changed drastically since I was a teenager. Now, people break up via email or texting instead of in-person. How does that affect girls, teenagers, and young women today? How does that affect dating? What things are happening out there in the world that interests young female writers? There are girl groups that are into outrageous and dangerous behavior. Groups of girls starve themselves, cut themselves, and put up nude videos of themselves on YouTube. What motivates them to do this? I think young women writers have an opportunity to tap into these issues and write about them. In fact *Thirteen*, written by Nikki Reed when she was in her teens and Catherine Hardwicke, was an incredibly powerful and heart-wrenching film that had an authenticity and insight that only someone who lived through that experience could capture. It was brilliantly acted by the young Evan Rachel Wood.

Another great personal story, *Nanny Diaries*, was written by two young women who revealed what it was like to work for super rich moms.

I don't mean to suggest that young female writers should only write about teen issues or their personal experiences, but those are areas where they have an advantage. I believe that a writer should write from the perspective that is uniquely theirs. In my case, I write from an Asian female perspective because that is the lens through which I view the world. There's no harm in trying to write outside of the person you are, but you have to be careful and do your research and immerse yourself in the culture you are writing within. Otherwise, your characters come off sounding contrived and ridiculous. So that's my advice: write what you know when you are starting out, because learning the craft of screenwriting is hard enough. You'll have more satisfying results with your first few screenplays if you write from the place you know best. After you get the craft down, then branch out.

Also, Hollywood tends to favor the young. Blockbusters are aimed at viewers in their late teens to mid-twenties. A writer from this age group could capture the spirit and style of this target audience quite well.

JS: You mentioned that you approach your projects from the perspective of an Asian American. How has being a minority affected your career? Do you have any advice for minority screenwriters who have recently begun their journey?

JL: Being a minority filmmaker has been both helpful and harmful, depending on the project. There are wonderful organizations out there that give voice to underrepresented communities. Organizations like the Independent Television Service (ITVS) and the Center for Asian American Media (CAAM) provided the means for me to make my scripts into finished films. Without them, my last two films wouldn't exist. The odds of getting supported through these types of organizations are much better than they would be for a screenplay competition. For instance, ITVS accepted 12 projects out of about 350 applicants the year that I got funded, and it was my fifth attempt with them. Those are still better odds than competing against a thousand screenplays in a competition. For CAAM, the odds were probably better than for ITVS. If you have a story that would fit the educational market stream, then going the non-profit funding route is probably your best option.

Now the downside of being a minority and female screenwriter. When I attended the American Film Market in 2007, I was very surprised and disappointed to be almost the only Asian I could see in the main part of the market. Ditto for the workshop and seminars being conducted by key people in the industry. At one particularly interesting workshop on pitching, the development executives that were there listened to about seven story pitches of IFP-sponsored projects. There were some amazing stories being developed by indie filmmakers. One of the stories being pitched was really quirky but sounded great. The development person admitted that although she personally loved quirky stories, there was no way she would financially support a script that was too far from a mainstream audience's taste. In this instance, I don't think anything was mentioned about a multi-cultural cast, although I think it was implied because the filmmaker was an Asian guy, as I recall. That was quite disheartening. That said, however, there was also a special forum for the Asian market during the AFM, predominantly attended by production houses and development heads from China, Hong Kong, and Korea for overseas production. Of course, that meant that pitched projects had to have relevance or interest for the viewers in these countries and to be under the censorship of their respective governments. The idea was to have some type of co-joint venture between two countries for producing a film. That can get tricky but it was a potential avenue. There wasn't anything I could see at the main section of the AFM for production or distribution of Asian-American themed films. I also got a chance to pitch to numerous development execs at a major studio earlier in 2000. It was clear that supporting a story written with strong Asian characters wasn't going to fly with them. I got a big wake up call during that whole process, but I haven't had any interactions with that world for a while.

There are other possibilities. I learned about Tribeca All Access only last year. They help kickstart feature narratives and filmmakers from underrepresented communities. And as I mentioned earlier, I learned about the A3 Sundance Fellowship two months ago and so I've just tried for both [Tribeca All Access and the A3 Sundance Fellowship] with my rom-com. I don't know how stiff the competition is, but I have a feeling there are a lot of us trying to get our scripts noticed. I also don't know how many of the films they support actually end up getting full funding, so it's a wait and see for now.

One hopeful trend I've been seeing within the last few years is that there are more actors of color on television: at least one in each television show I've tuned into. That is a huge change. Perhaps things are slowly opening up. I certainly hope so.

JS: So many uphill battles, it seems; but it is good to hear people are trying to make a difference. Thank you again for sharing your story and for the wonderful pieces of advice! Do you have any other pieces of advice you would like to share? Any thoughts on the future of the industry? One sentence that says it all?

JL: Thank you for allowing me to share my long-winded stories. My parting words: You have to believe in your project in the face of naysayers and obstacles. That faith in your creative vision is what keeps you moving forward, so continue to put your work out there because there is an audience for it.

PART THREE: STORY STRUCTURE

It is not for me to say which structure you should follow, but I would like to provide a quick commentary on structure so you are better prepared to make an educated decision. To really know what you are talking about, you should study each of these structure styles. You may find you have to look to one of these every time you outline a story. You may find them useful after writing as a way to go back and assess your story, and you may decide to create a Frankenstein style of your own. Stephan Bugaj says in his interview in Part Four that you should read the books so that when you are in meetings with people who have read them, you will understand the terms being thrown around. Anthony Burch agrees, as he says in his interview in Part Five to study these "so you can speak the language of people who have read *Save the Cat* but who don't actually know what legitimately makes stories work."

The main types of structure that people talk about are laid out in such books as *Save the Cat: The Last Book on Screenwriting You'll Ever Need*, by Blake Snyder; *The Writer's Journey: Mythic Structure for Writers*, by Christopher Vogler; and *Screenwriting: The Sequence Approach*, by Paul Gulino. One that is not in book format but that may have something to offer you is called the "Seven Point Story Structure." These are the structures discussed in this section, though there are many more. You may have heard of "The Mini Movie Method," which I chose not to include because of its lack of popularity in my circles. Still, you may find it useful and it is worth looking it up to see what you think. Likewise you may have heard of the book *Screenplay: The Foundations of Screenwriting*, by Syd Field, and wonder why I did not include it below. Syd Field's book, while a must read, basically says there are three acts to a screenplay (or any story). Screenplay should be read by any aspiring screenwriter, but I would say it is more about fundamental knowledge and less about a style of screenplay structure.

These methods have much in common, and many of them are based on Joseph *Campbell's The Hero's Journey*. None of them should be seen as rules. As I have stressed and continue to stress, these should be seen as guides to help you craft your story. Remember, this is your story, so stay true to what your story needs to be. Do not ruin it by changing everything to fit into some story mold. That said, some people will disagree with me and say that these are indeed rules (some of the books even say so). You will have to make that decision for yourself.

Structure can be just as important in your novel writing and video game writing as in screenwriting. For screenwriting in particular, we need structure to get past the first line of defense when submitting our screenplays – those readers who may have less experience than we do, but who we must get past in order to have our screenplays read by the more experienced readers and professionals in the industry. You are a sniper; you need to get close enough to take the shot—but those darn walls of soldiers are standing in your way.

Having written numerous screenplays and worked professionally as a creative writer, I can say I have played with structure. I started by adapting one of my novels into a monster that only slightly resembled a screenplay, transitioned into a style of writing that closely mirrored *The Hero's Journey* or *Save the Cat* patterns, and in one or two more recent stories I took artistic license and wrote whatever the heck I felt like.

When you finish a story, the next step is to figure out what to do with it. By "finish" I mean it has been workshopped and rewritten and all that. For me it generally involves a series of contest submissions (Nicholl, Austin, Page), queries through

IMDb Pro when I have a free trial, or maybe a mass query service like ScriptVenice. When you reach a certain level of success in your career, you may simply send your script to your manager or agent. Maybe you go back and re-craft your script to make sure it fits the rules, or re-read *Story: Style, Structure, Substance, and the Principles of Screenwriting*, by Robert McKee, and make sure your story follows his guidelines.

If you have yet to land yourself an agent or manager, those pesky readers are often waiting to tell you that you forgot to include *Save the Cat* step 13 or whatever. Yet in panels at the Writers Guild Foundation, the Austin Film Festival, and in many blogs, we often hear that books on screenwriting are worthless, and that the structure rules from *The Hero's Journey* or *Save the Cat* are for wannabes and produce predictable stories. The artist inside you should be smart enough to know when to bend the so called rules. I believe it was Ashley Miller (*Thor, X-Men: First Class*) at the Austin Film Festival 2012 who advised aspiring writers to read the books and then throw them away.

How do we tackle the readers who insist that X has to happen on page 12 and Y has to follow X? Do we follow Charlie Kaufman's route (the character in his movie *Adaptation*, not the actual amazing writer) and go to a Robert McKee story seminar and make our screenplay fit the structure so that it sells? The optimal answer is to have two versions of one script—the first for those lovely readers who will be judging your text based solely on superficial structure, the second for the people who will actually make the film. At the end of the day, film making is such a collaborative process that the film may become super predictable regardless of how you started off structuring your story.

Stay loyal to the artist in you, but be conscious of what the readers and gurus are preaching. When it makes your script better, listen to them. But the artist always comes first.

In the following section I have included an example in each

section from *Teddy Bears in Monsterland*, a story of mine that started as a screenplay and became a novel (for ages 7-12), and could also be a fun video game, in theory. This story works for our purpose because it translates across the media discussed in this book. You may want to read the book before continuing on, but if you have not had the chance, I include ample information for you to follow along. For reference purposes, and to show you how similar the approaches of the structures really are, I chose to include the examples under each section at the risk of being repetitive. If you would like more examples from other stories, a Google search will bring up examples of these structures applied to *Star Wars* and other movies and games. Try searching for "Beat Sheet, Star Wars."

Each section has references within the structure formats for how each point relates to the points in the other structures. If there is no direct relation, that section is left blank. As you see how each section relates, or does not, you may find that a combination of these and possibly other structures is what works best for you.

Save the Cat

Early on in my screenwriting studies I came across the book *Save the Cat: The Last Book on Screenwriting You'll Ever Need*. Practically everyone at a small film festival I was attending referred to this book, so I decided to look it up. I devoured the book in a day while at the court waiting to see if I would be used for jury duty. The book gets its title from the idea that movies often resort to the protagonist doing something nice at the beginning so the viewers will like him or her early on, such as saving the cat. Is it a perfect book? No. Is it a fun and easy read? Yes. But *Save the Cat* is one of those books that tries to prescribe rules, so proceed with caution. One particular rule in this book is that the main points happen on (or around, if loosely translated) specific pages. I have left these pages out of my summary, because I do no ascribe to such rules and think they can be harmful.

The structure presented in *Save the Cat,* also known as the "Blake Snyder Beat Sheet" is as follows:

Opening Image: A visual that sets the tone, mood, and style of the movie. The opening image should introduce the protagonist and show a snapshot of the protagonist before the journey. Most of all, it should cause the viewers or readers to be excited about what is to come.

Theme Stated: Usually in the early portion of your story, someone will implicitly or explicitly state the theme. This can often come in the form of a question. It is fine, and probably even encouraged, for the protagonist to not understand the comment at the time, but readers and viewers will certainly see the protagonist come to learn its importance.

Set-up: Including the above sections, the first portion of the story should set up the protagonist, the goal, and the stakes. Here we should meet every main character of the A story, plant the protagonist's tics and behaviors, and show how and why the protagonist will transform if they hope to win. The steps up to and including the Set-up correlate to the Ordinary World from *The Writer's Journey*, Sequence A from *The Sequence Approach*, and The Hook from the "Seven Point Story Structure."

Catalyst: Now is the time to bring a change to this world of the story, the moment that throws your protagonist on his or her head and challenges them to make a change. This is the Call to Adventure from *The Writer's Journey*, what ends Sequence A in *The Sequence Approach*, and the Plot Turn 1 from the "Seven Point Story Structure."

Debate: As change never comes easy, this is where the protagonist considers how horrible it would be to follow this new path, but how much worse it would be to do nothing. The protagonist asks if he or she is willing to do what it takes, the answer being that they have to try. This is the Refusal of the Call from *The Writer's Journey*, Sequence B from *The Sequence Approach*.

Break into Two: The protagonist has made a choice and leaves the old world behind, entering a new world (whether this is an actual physical new world or a new state of being). This must be a decision that the protagonist makes. This is basically the Crossing the First Threshold from *The Writer's Journey*, the end of Sequence B in *The Sequence Approach*.

B Story: This is the story that carries the theme of the movie, and is often in the form of a love story. While not in the same order, this is similar to Sequence E in *The Sequence Approach*, and relates to the allies section of Tests, Allies, and Enemies in *The Writer's Journey*.

Fun and Games: This is the fun part of the story, the part where we deliver on the premise. If this is a movie, it is where most of the movie trailer moments will come from, or the "set pieces." I disagree with one main point here, which is that Blake Snyder says the stakes will not be raised until the midpoint, but if you choose to be a *Save the Cat* person, that can be your call. This is similar to the Tests, Allies, and Enemies as well as the Approach to the Innermost Cave in *The Writer's Journey*, Sequences C and D from *The Sequence Approach*, and would likely include the Pinch 1 from "Seven Point Story Structure."

Midpoint: The midpoint is where we see either a false victory or a false defeat. In my discussions with Jeremy Breslau, interviewed in this book, I came to see either of these moments as coming close before or after a moment with the opposite feeling – a false defeat will come immediately after a false victory. It is up to you as the author to decide what your true midpoint is. What matters is that the stakes are raised and the fun and games are over. Blake Snyder also says this moment is the opposite of the All is Lost moment, so if you go with a false victory here, then that moment should be a false defeat. The midpoint resembles The Ordeal from *The Writer's Journey*, the end of Sequence D in *The Sequence Approach*, and the aptly named Midpoint from the "Seven Point Story Structure."

Bad Guys Close In: Here is where writers often have the hardest time. This is where, although the protagonist may have thought he or she was in the clear at the midpoint, the bad guys bring the pain. It is also where our protagonist faces doubt and, if part of a group, jealousy and internal dissent. This has similarities to The Road Back in *The Writer's Journey*, and may be encapsulated in Sequence F of *The Sequence Approach*.

All is Lost: This may be the opposite moment from the midpoint, but I will stress my argument that this should always feel like total defeat. Blake Snyder puts a "whiff of death" in this section, where someone dies or almost dies, in a way that reminds the viewers that death for the protagonist is indeed possible. This means that the old world and way of thinking dies as well, and the protagonist feels the All is Lost moment that much more. This point relates to the death aspect of The Resurrection in *The Writer's Journey*, falls somewhere in Sequence G of *The Sequence Approach*, and combined with the Dark Night of the Soul below makes up the Pinch 2 in "Seven Point Story Structure."

Dark Night of the Soul: This is "the darkness right before the dawn." It is the moment when, after losing everything, the protagonist feels hopeless and helpless, and sees no way forward. This falls in Sequence G of *The Sequence Approach*.

Break into Three: Here the protagonist gets back up, using everything learned throughout the story to make a comeback. This is the rebirth section of The Resurrection in *The Writer's Journey*, the end of Sequence G in *The Sequence Approach*, and seems to be the Plot Turn 2 in "Seven Point Story Structure."

Finale: In Act Three the protagonist will tie up all loose ends, applying the lessons learned, mastering any character tics, and bringing the A story and B story to a triumphant end. Through dealing with the problem, the protagonist leaves the old world behind and brings in a "new world order." This is similar to the Return with the Elixir in *The Writer's Journey*, Sequence H in *The Sequence Approach*, and the Resolution in "Seven Point Story Structure."

Final Image: In a stunning closing image, we see the opposite of the opening image and prove visually that the change has occurred and that it is real.

Example of how *Save the Cat* is used with *Teddy Bears in Monsterland:*

Opening Image: Rick plays with his teddy bear, Fluffy, simulating a fight while watching monster cartoons.

Theme Stated: Rick's mom tells him he shouldn't be afraid of the dark, and that maybe he is too grown up to have a teddy bear.

Set-up: When Rick falls asleep, Fluffy ensures they are safe but we see that he too is afraid of the dark. What he first thinks is a monster is just a mouse. He has a close call with Rick waking up, and we see the dynamic of teddy bears protecting their children by coming alive at night.

Catalyst: Real monsters show up! Fluffy tries to fight them off with the light he pulls from the nightlight, but it's not enough. He watches helpless as the monsters disappear with Rick into the shadows.

Debate: Fluffy runs for help and tries to get Rick's mom, but it does not work. Rick's mom's old teddy bear tells Fluffy that it's like the old legends, when the monsters and teddy bears were at war. If Fluffy wants to save Rick, he'll have to go through the attic to find the teddy bear elders.

Break into Two: Fluffy is not sure about the mission because he is too scared, but then he hears Rick's sister scream and finds she too has been taken by the monsters. If he does not act, all the kids may be taken! He goes to the attic and finds a ghoul that opens the door to the teddy bear picnic, where the elders reside.

B Story: This moment in my story comes a bit later, when a pink bear, who has never had anyone of her own, is reluctant to risk helping Fluffy find Rick.

Fun and Games: Fluffy faces all sorts of problems, starting with being exiled for spreading rumors about the return of the monsters. No one believes Fluffy. He is sent to a land of desert and tossed away teddy bears. These gruff teddy bears make Fluffy fight in the pits to prove himself. But when the monsters arrive, everyone flees and Fluffy finds himself allied with a kind of ninja bear and the pink bear. They escape the monsters and the ninja bear takes Fluffy to a haunted fortress.

Midpoint: Fluffy survives the fortress and the ninja bear leads Fluffy to the basement, the entrance to the shadowlands where the monsters have Rick.

Bad Guys Close In: As Fluffy descends into the shadowlands with his companions, he sees that the children are being turned into monsters.

All is Lost: Fluffy and his crew reach the last level of the shadowlands, but when the pink bear sees her brother trapped by the monsters she tries to go after him. Fluffy says they need a strategy, trying to pull her back. She is worked up and shoves him back, causing him to fall off a cliff. He recovers at the bottom to find the ninja bear helped break his fall, but feels it is all over.

Dark Night of the Soul: The ninja bear enters a pool of shimmering darkness, the path monsters take to enter the shadows of our homes. Now Fluffy is all alone. How can he escape this? How can he prevent Rick from turning into a monster?

Break into Three: After Fluffy escapes to save Rick and reveal a plot against children led by the elder bear who exiled Fluffy, Fluffy convinces the monsters to help fight to save the children. He summons light from his heart, his paw in Rick's, and they go through a tunnel of light.

Finale: The teddy bear elder and his grizzly bear warriors fight Fluffy and his friends, which now include the monsters. Fluffy's side wins and order is restored, but now the monsters agree to get help from the teddy bears and learn how to have fun with the children. Rick and his sister agree to help them along the way.

Final Image: Rick realizes he does not need Fluffy to overcome his fear of the dark, and gives Fluffy to his sister, along with the two teddy bears who accompanied Fluffy on his journey. Rick removes his night light and places it on his bed stand before going to sleep on his own.

The Writer's Journey

A writing partner once recommended we prepare our story with *The Writer's Journey: Mythic Structure for Writers* structure in mind. This book changed my life, and I loved it. It is largely based on Joseph Campbell's *The Hero's Journey*. I promptly went out and bought more of Campbell's work, including an old book on mythology that I loved. His work highly influenced my first novel. *The Writer's Journey* was also one of the only books that one of my most respected literary writing professors recommended, and now I pass that recommendation on to you. You may particularly enjoy this structure if you love traditional sword and sorcery tales.

The stages of *The Writer's Journey* are as follows:

The Ordinary World: We meet the protagonist and see their everyday life. This is the Set-Up from *Save the Cat*, Sequence A from *The Sequence Approach*, and the Hook from the "Seven Point Story Structure."

The Call to Adventure: The protagonist's world is thrown upside down, throwing the story into action. This is the Catalyst from *Save the Cat*, what ends Sequence A in *The Sequence Approach*, and the Plot Turn 1 from the "Seven Point Story Structure."

Refusal of the Call: The protagonist debates whether and how to answer the call. This is the Debate from *Save the Cat*, and Sequence B from *The Sequence Approach*.

Meeting with the Mentor: The protagonist gains the supplies, knowledge, and confidence needed to accept the call and go on the adventure.

Crossing the First Threshold: The protagonist commits wholeheartedly to the adventure, breaking into the second act. This is the Break into Two from *Save the Cat*, and the end of Sequence B in *The Sequence Approach*.

Tests, Allies and Enemies: The protagonist explores the special world, faces trials, and makes friends and enemies. This is the fun and games section. This relates to the B Story and Fun and Games from *Save the Cat*, Sequence C from *The Sequence Approach*, and likely includes the Pinch 1 from "Seven Point Story Structure."

Approach to the Innermost Cave: The protagonist nears the center of the story and the special world. This is more Fun and Games from *Save the Cat*, and Sequence D from *The Sequence Approach*.

The Ordeal: The protagonist faces the greatest challenge yet and experiences death and rebirth. This seems to be another word for the Midpoint in *Save the Cat* and "Seven Point Story Structure," and is seen at the end of Sequence D in *The Sequence Approach*.

Reward: The hero experiences the consequences of surviving death.

The Road Back: The protagonist returns to the ordinary world or continues to an ultimate destination. This has similarities to Bad Guys Close in from *Save the Cat*, and Sequence E and F in *The Sequence Approach*.

The Resurrection: The protagonist experiences a final moment of death and rebirth so he or she is pure when he or she reenters the ordinary world. The death moment here goes along with the All is Lost and Dark Night of the Soul moments from *Save the Cat*, the end of Sequence F in *The Sequence Approach*, and the Pinch 2 from "Seven Point Story Structure." The rebirth moment goes along with the Break into Three in *Save the Cat*, the end of Sequence G in *The Sequence Approach*, and Plot Turn 2 in "Seven Point Story Structure."

Return with the Elixir: The protagonist returns to improve the ordinary world. This is basically the Finale from *Save the Cat*, the Sequence H in *The Sequence Approach*, and the Resolution in "Seven Point Story Structure."

Example of how *The Writer's Journey* is used with *Teddy Bears in Monsterland*:

The Ordinary World: Rick plays with his teddy bear and we see the dynamic of teddy bears protecting their children by coming alive at night.

The Call to Adventure: Real monsters show up! Fluffy tries to fight them off with the light he pulls from the nightlight, but it is not enough. He watches helpless as the monsters disappear with Rick into the shadows.

Refusal of the Call: Fluffy runs for help and tries to get Rick's mom, but it does not work. He does not know what to do.

Meeting with the Mentor: Rick's mom's old teddy bear tells Fluffy that it is like the old legends, when the monsters and teddy bears were at war. If Fluffy wants to save Rick, he will have to go through the attic to find the teddy bear elders.

Crossing the First Threshold: When Fluffy hears Rick's sister scream and finds she too has been taken by the monsters, he commits to the journey. He goes to the attic and finds a ghoul that opens the door to the teddy bear picnic, where the elders reside.

Tests, Allies, and Enemies: Fluffy faces all sorts of problems, starting with the fact that one of the teddy bear elders exiles him for spreading rumors about the return of the monsters. No one believes Fluffy. He is sent to a land of desert and tossed away teddy bears, where he is picked on and still not believed. But when the monsters arrive, everyone flees and

Fluffy finds himself allied with a kind of ninja bear and a pink bear.

Approach the Innermost Cave: They escape the monsters and the ninja bear reveals that he can take Fluffy through a haunted fortress to where Rick is being held captive.

The Ordeal: Fluffy survives the fortress and the ninja bear leads Fluffy to the basement, the entrance to the shadowlands where the monsters have Rick.

Reward: Fluffy survives the obstacles in his way with the help of the ninja bear and pink bear, whose friendship he earned in the fortress.

The Road Back: As Fluffy descends into the shadowlands with his companions, he sees that the children are being turned into monsters. Fluffy and his crew fight monsters and Fluffy is separated and left all alone. He discovers a larger plot led by the teddy bear elder, and learns that the monsters were misguided.

The Resurrection: Fluffy, now with the bears and monsters fight the elder bear, but seems about to lose. Rick overcomes his fright of the dark and stands by Fluffy's side. Together they are unstoppable. They win and order is restored.

Return with the Elixir: The monsters agree to get help from the teddy bears and learn how to have fun with the children. Rick and his sister agree to help them along the way. Rick realizes he does not need Fluffy to overcome his fear of the dark, and gives Fluffy to his sister, along with the two teddy bears who accompanied Fluffy on his journey. Rick removes his nightlight and places it on his bed stand before going to sleep on his own.

The Sequence Approach

When you research USC you will see their screenwriting program is knowne for *The Sequence Approach* (see Jeremy Breslau's interview for some more talk about USC being awesome). This approach was developed by Frank Daniel while he was the head of the USC Graduate Screenwriting Program, and is discussed in great detail in Paul Gulino's book, Screenwriting: *The Sequence Approach*. The "Go into the Story" blog (one we should all follow) also did a wonderful job covering this approach. It works particularly well for people who want to think in chunks, instead of specific beats to hit on specific page numbers. For those of you that wonder "What do I make happen between the Approach to the Innermost Cave and The Ordeal, this structure may be for you. Screenwriting: *The Sequence Approach* breaks the screenplay into eight sequences of twelve to fifteen pages each (for a screenplay – for a novel, consider these as percentages).

The stages of *The Sequence Approach* are as follows:

Sequence A: The first section, much like the other first sections, sets up the story with who, what, when, where, and the hook. We get a glimpse of the protagonist's life before the actual story begins, and we should see a hint of how that life would have turned out if the story did not get interrupted as it will when the point of attack or inciting incident comes and forces the protagonist into action. This encapsulates up through the Set-up and ends with the Catalyst from *Save the Cat*, includes The Ordinary world to the The Call to Adventure from *The Writer's Journey*, and the Hook to the Plot Turn 1 from "Seven Point Story Structure."

Sequence B: The second section generally sets up the main tension and poses the dramatic question that shapes the remainder of the story. This sequence is where the protagonist struggles with the change brought about by the inciting incident. This sequence goes until the end of the first act. This is the Debate from *Save the Cat*, and the Refusal of the Call and possibly the Meeting with the Mentor from *The Writer's Journey*.

Sequence C: Starting the second act, the third sequence is where the protagonist first attempts to solve the problem left dangling at the end of Sequence B. While the protagonist may solve an immediate problem here and throughout the story, this resolution will lead to a bigger and deeper problem. This is the Break into Two through part of the Fun and Games from *Save the Cat*, Crossing the First Threshold and some of Tests, Allies and Enemies from *The Writer's Journey*, and likely ends with the Pinch 1 from "Seven Point Story Structure."

Sequence D: Here the first attempt to solve the problem fails and we see the protagonist increase their effort to find a way back to a normal life. This often leads to the midpoint of the film, often as a reversal of fortune in a way that gives the reader or audience hope, only to squash said hope. This includes the rest of Fun and Games from *Save the Cat*, the rest of Tests, Allies, and Enemies as well as the Approach to the Innermost Cave from *The Writer's Journey*, and leads to the Midpoint or Ordeal in *Save the Cat*, *The Sequence Approach*, and "Seven Point Story Structure."

Sequence E: Now the protagonist must work to resolve the problem that arose in Sequence D, and may be the point in the story where new characters are introduced. This may correlate to the B story in *Save the Cat* (though listed in a different order), and included in the Reward or Road Back in *The Writer's Journey*.

Sequence F: In the last sequence of the second act, the protagonist has eliminated all easy potential solutions to the problem. Gulino states that this does not need to end in a low point, but often promotes an emotion opposite of that of the ending. This relates to the Bad Guys Close In point in *Save the Cat*, the Reward and The Road Back from *The Writer's Journey*, and likely includes the Pinch 2 point from "Seven Point Story Structure."

Sequence G: While it may seem the final resolution occurs here, it is a false resolution that brings unexpected consequences. The story can be turned upside down here, with higher stakes and a quickened pace. The resolution of this sequence is often characterized by a reversal. This point likely includes All is Lost and Dark Night of the Soul, and Break into Three from *Save the Cat*, The Resurrection from *The Writer's Journey*, and the Plot Turn 2 from "Seven Point Story Structure."

Sequence H: Finally, the chaos that started with the inciting incident is settled, for better or worse. This is the resolution, where any loose ends are tied up. This point is the Finale in *Save the Cat*, Return with the Elixir in *The Writer's Journey*, and the Resolution from "Seven Point Story Structure."

Example of how *The Sequence Approach* is used with *Teddy Bears in Monsterland*:

Sequence A: Rick plays with his teddy bear and we see the dynamic of teddy bears protecting their children by coming alive at night. Real monsters show up! Fluffy tries to fight them off with the light he pulls from the nightlight, but it's not enough. He watches helpless as the monsters disappear with Rick into the shadows.

Sequence B: Fluffy runs for help and tries to get Rick's mom, but it does not work. When Fluffy hears Rick's sister scream and finds she too has been taken by the monsters, he commits to the journey. He goes to the attic and finds a ghoul that opens the door to the teddy bear picnic, where the elders reside.

Sequence C: Fluffy faces all sorts of problems, starting with the fact that one of the teddy bear elders exiles him for spreading rumors about the return of the monsters. No one believes Fluffy. He is sent to a land of desert and tossed away teddy bears, where he is picked on and still not believed. But when the monsters arrive, everyone flees and Fluffy finds himself allied with a kind of ninja bear and a pink bear.

Sequence D: They escape the monsters and the ninja bear reveals he can take Fluffy through a haunted fortress to the basement and the entrance of the shadowlands, where the monsters will have Rick.

Sequence E: Fluffy enters the shadowlands and survives the obstacles in his way with the help of the ninja bear and pink bear, whose friendship he earned in the fortress.

Sequence F: As Fluffy descends into the shadowlands with his companions, he sees that the children are being turned into monsters. Fluffy and his crew fight monsters and Fluffy is separated and left all alone. He discovers a larger plot led by the teddy bear elder, and learns that the monsters were misguided as he befriends one of them.

Sequence G: Fluffy, now with the bears and monsters fight the elder bear, but seems about to lose. Rick overcomes his fright of the dark and stands by Fluffy's side. Together they are unstoppable. They win and order is restored.

Sequence H: The monsters agree to get help from the teddy bears and learn how to have fun with the children. Rick and his sister agree to help them along the way. Rick realizes he does not need Fluffy to overcome his fear of the dark, and gives Fluffy to his sister, along with the two teddy bears who accompanied Fluffy on his journey. Rick removes his nightlight and places it on his bed stand before going to sleep on his own.

Seven Point Story Structure with Dan Wells

Dan Wells is a co-star on one of my favorite fiction writing podcasts, titled "Writing Excuses." Wells gleaned the "Seven Point Story Structure," from an old *Star Trek* RPG guidebook. Lucky for you, his talk on structure is available on YouTube and he has posted the video and PowerPoint for your downloading pleasure on his website. What makes it even more fun is that Wells uses examples from *Star Wars* and Harry Potter.

This structure is as follows:

Hook: This is where your protagonist starts from. You set up your protagonist's world and set their stakes (what they have to lose) in this part. This correlates to everything up through the Set-up in *Save the Cat*, The Ordinary World in *The Writer's Journey*, and Sequence A in *The Sequence Approach*.

Plot Turn 1: This is the event that sets your story in motion. It moves you from the beginning to the Midpoint. Your protagonist's world changes here. This is the Catalyst in *Save the Cat*, the Call to Adventure in *The Writer's Journey*, and comes at the end of Sequence A in *The Sequence Approach*.

Pinch 1: Pinches are where you put pressure on your protagonist from your antagonist to force your protagonist into action. Wells says this is the point where the author applies pressure in a way that forces the protagonist into action, which often comes in the form of bad guys attacking. This happens somewhere in Fun and Games in *Save the Cat*, the Tests, Allies, and Enemies section of *The Writer's Journey*, and within Sequence C or D of *The Sequence Approach*.

Midpoint: The midpoint takes your protagonist from reaction to action. At the midpoint, your protagonist determines that she must do something. (This can take place over a series of scenes.) This is the Midpoint from *Save the Cat*, The Ordeal from *The Writer's Journey*, and comes at the end of Sequence D in *The Sequence Approach*.

Pinch 2: Pinch 2 is where your story takes the ultimate dive. Your protagonist is sitting in the jaws of defeat. Everything has fallen apart. This relates to All is Lost and Dark Night of the Soul in *Save the Cat*, the death portion of The Resurrection from *The Writer's Journey*, and falls in Sequence F in *The Sequence Approach*.

Plot Turn 2: This point moves the story from the Midpoint to the Resolution. Plot Turn 2 is where your protagonist receives the final piece of information that he needs to make it to the resolution. (No new information can be introduced after this point.) Your protagonist finally understands he has the power to achieve the resolution. This relates to Break into Three in *Save the Cat*, The Resurrection in *The Writer's Journey*, and Sequence G of *The Sequence Approach*.

Resolution: Your protagonist completes what he sets out to do. This is the Finale in *Save the Cat*, the Return with the Elixir in *The Writer's Journey*, and Sequence H in *The Sequence Approach*.

When you are done watching Dan's video and looking over his slides, start listening to the "Writing Excuses" podcast. There is so much to learn in the podcast's 15 minute sessions.

Example of how "The Seven Point Story Structure" is used with *Teddy Bears in Monsterland*:

Hook: Rick plays with his teddy bear and we see the dynamic of teddy bears protecting their children by coming alive at night.

Plot Turn 1: Real monsters show up! Fluffy tries to fight them off with the light he pulls from the nightlight, but it is not enough. He watches helpless as the monsters disappear with Rick into the shadows.

Pinch 1: One of the teddy bear elders exiles Fluffy for spreading rumors about the return of the monsters. No one believes Fluffy. He is sent to a land of desert and tossed away teddy bears.

Midpoint: The other bears make Fluffy fight, but disperse when monsters show up. Fluffy finds himself allied with a kind of ninja bear and a pink bear. The ninja bear says he can take Fluffy through a haunted fortress to the basement and the entrance of the shadowlands, where the monsters will have Rick.

Pinch 2: Fluffy and his crew reach the last level of the shadowlands, but when the pink bear sees her brother trapped by the monsters she tries to go after him. Fluffy says they need a strategy, but she is worked up and shoves him back, causing him to fall off a cliff.

Plot Turn 2: Fluffy is ready to save Rick, the fight back on with the help of a flying monster. But when they arrive, they find the teddy bear elder conspiring with the orc king! All the teddy bears have been taken prisoner, and Rick is among them.

Resolution: Fluffy's side wins and order is restored, but now the monsters agree to get help from the teddy bears and learn how to have fun with the children. Rick and his sister agree to help them along the way. Rick realizes he does not need Fluffy to overcome his fear of the dark, and gives Fluffy to his sister, along with the two teddy bears who are Fluffy's companions from the journey. Rick removes his night light and places it on his bed stand before going to sleep on his own.

Part Three Next Steps

If you have already written something without thinking about the above structures, try applying one of them to your story. What is your inciting incident or first pinch? Does your opening image contrast with your closing image? Reassess your story to see if you can improve it. This retroactive application of structure has always been helpful to me. It may not result in large changes, instead sometimes leading me to realize that the characters' emotions could be amped up at certain points to play with the audience expectations, but it's a way of looking at your writing from a new perspective— which is always helpful. If you do not have a story of your own, try analyzing one of your favorite stories and according to each of the above structures, and then start brainstorming your next story with your favorite structure in mind. The result may surprise you.

My Story Structure Plan

1. Which of the outlined structures resonates for me?

2. What story of my own (or of someone else's) would I like to analyze with this structure?

3. Based on the analysis, what changes might I make to this story? If none, why not?

4. How would a story that I come up with using any of the above structures differ from stories I have brainstormed in the past?

Interview: Bob Saenz, Screenwriting Outside of LA

Bob Saenz, an actor, screenwriter, and all-around great guy has some advice for those of us trying to make our first sell. If you are struggling with structure, or if you already know you are not a structure nut, you will enjoy his thoughts on the subject. He shares his encouraging words for those of us screenwriters who do not live in LA but want to work writing screenplays, and also talks about adapting a book into a screenplay.

***

Justin Sloan: You have proven that you don't have to live in Los Angeles to write screenplays. Do you feel this can be attributed to any one aspect of your career or one choice you've made?

Bob Saenz: Yes. I don't want to live there. Easy as that. I love the Bay Area. It's my home and with Skype and email and conference calls and Southwest Airlines at my beck and call, I've never had anyone blink twice that I live here instead of LA. Doesn't mean it will always be that way, but so far so good. I've only had to be in LA the next day once, and I made the meeting. Oh... I also wrote good scripts that people wanted and where I lived didn't matter as long as I had those.

JS: That is cool you have been able to make it work. Like you said, the good script is key. I understand you have acted as well. How much do you feel your acting has helped with your craft as a writer? How much has it helped with the networking to establish yourself as a writer? Did you act only in the Bay Area, or did you live in Los Angeles at some point?

BS: Yes, I started out as an actor. I'm a 20 year SAG-AFTRA

member. Being on sets has helped me as a writer more than being an actor (I'm not that great an actor anyway). And I've been lucky to have been on sets as an actor, both film and TV, with some iconic directors and actors—and kept my mouth shut, for the most part, and my eyes open and gotten an amazing education on how film and TV operate. And yes, the networking I did on those sets was crucial to my writing getting seen by the right people. I've been fortunate to have never sent a query letter to anyone. Most of my acting jobs were here in the Bay Area, but I have been hired to act in LA films and gone there to do it. Fortunately for the viewing public, I'm not acting much anymore. Too busy with writing jobs, thank you God.

JS: I am sure the viewing public misses you. As someone who has acted and now writes, I completely agree that sometimes writing can be more fulfilling. I understand you have adapted fiction and non-fiction works for the screen. What is the biggest challenge of doing this? I have considered approaching one of my published friends about such an endeavor. Would you advise aspiring writers try this as another way to get a foot in the door?

BS: It's a fabulous experience and one that any writer hoping to do this should try at some point. I've adapted a non-fiction book, working with the author to make sure I did it justice and adapted a novel without the author's help. Both times I had to learn to combine events and plot points and characters, add scenes and characters, delete subplots, you name it.... all to make a book fit a two-hour viewing window and try to not lose the original material. And if you have the rights to a great book and can turn out a great script based on it, YES... it can be another way through the door. I optioned the rights to a story that was in the newspapers all over the world last year.

JS: IMDb shows your movie Help for the Holidays came

out in 2012 and Extracurricular Activities is in production. That is very exciting! How many scripts did you write to get to this point? Are you willing to share any particularly interesting adventures you have had along the way?

BS: Help for the Holidays was a Hallmark Channel Christmas film in 2012. It was the number-one-rated original film on Hallmark in 2012 and the number-ten-rated Hallmark film of all time. It did help that Summer Glau starred in it, but it was an unqualified hit for Hallmark. And didn't hurt me much with them either.

And I just got a director's cut last week of *Cupid's Bed & Breakfast*, the next film I wrote for Hallmark. A romantic comedy/drama that's not as cutesy as the title might make you think. It's not even on IMDb yet, but will be soon. I am unbelievably happy with the way the film turned out.

I sold them another original script, *The Right Girl*, a romantic comedy that I wrote with my good friend (and great writer) Jeff Willis. We did six paid rewrites and it shot in July 2014. And *Extracurricular Activities* is scheduled to shoot in February 2015, but as we all know, that is subject to change. It's a theatrical film. One that will be released to theaters. Hopefully, a lot of theaters. I'm really happy with the well-known actors involved, so far, but can't say anything public yet about it. I've optioned two other original scripts this year and have a dozen other projects tap-dancing out there for next year.

And all this wasn't an overnight thing. It's taken close to 20 years. Lots of rejection and lots of incredible heartbreaking moments when something almost got made but didn't and lots of fakes and charlatans along the way who prey on new writers (luckily I got good really fast at spotting them), and through it all I never gave up. I have a couple of dozen scripts and four original pilots all ready to go and ideas on my white board for many more scripts, including two true stories.

And this week, signed a contract to write an episode of a new hour long cable network series for the fall... can't tell you what it is yet, but will be able to in the near future I think. And... a couple of really good and successful directors who say they have ideas for me when I come up for air.

JS: You seem to have a talent for writing movies that are contained, meaning there are no aliens blowing up the world or massive car chases. Is this part of your strategy? Do you have any words of wisdom to share with aspiring screenwriters regarding this?

BS: There's a very good reason for this. Big movies can only be sold to four or five people in the industry. Small films can be sold to a whole lot more. I've chosen to go after the better opportunity. I always have a budget in mind before I even start a script, so I know I have to write a great script within those numbers. It works for me. Producers can always make something bigger as they develop a script. I've found they don't buy something with the idea of cutting it back. It's easier to sell a lower budget film. It's a fact. Oh... I do have a very funny massive car chase in one of my scripts, but then it's one where I said, "To hell with the budget." But it's the only one of my originals with that kind of budget; all the other ones are a lot smaller.

JS: In your writing, do you follow any particular method? Is there a book on structure that you follow and would recommend, and if so (or not), why?

BS: I have never read a book on structure. Doesn't mean there may not be some good ones out there, but it has always seemed to me that by sticking to one structure guide or another you rob yourself of the freedom of taking your story where it needs to go organically, even if you have outlined it. Good stories are living breathing things, and a good writer, who knows his or her characters well, will recognize when his or her characters need to take the story in an unplanned direction. If you rely on the structure books, you're less inclined to take these organic twists and turns that could be the things that make your script special.

JS: For aspiring writers, what do you think is the most important point to remember when bombarded with all of these different books on structure, screenwriting gurus claiming they have all the answers, and everyone else (such as us) giving them advice?

BS: Once again: Write. Read scripts from films you like. Read bad scripts. Write. Write. And then write more. There certainly are things to be learned from pro writers. My own blog is filled with advice for the new writer, but no one has all the answers. No one has most of the answers. Each writer has to develop his or her own style, his or her own voice in his or her work. That's what sets you apart. And the only way to find that voice is to write and write until you find it. Sometimes it's on script three. Sometimes it's on script fifteen. Sometimes it's never found.

JS: Finally, do you have any other advice to other screenwriters outside of LA who want to get established without relocating?

BS: Keep at it. Write. Write. Write. Read good scripts and see how it's done. Read awful scripts and see how it's not done. Write. Write. And write. Don't give up. And when you think you have that one great script, get a manager. Query your manager with it. My manager, who I got on a referral from a director, has made a world of difference to my career. And that success all came from one script I wrote, which everyone loves in Hollywood: *Extracurricular Activities*. And I never told people I lived in Northern California before they read it. They never asked and I never told them. Afterward, it didn't matter. Oh, and you need to have money to get back and forth to LA. I go every other month or so for a week at a time. It can be expensive.

Interview: Chris Jalufka, Evil Tender

Chris Jalufka is a former script reader and collector of other production and post- production jobs in the film and advertising industries. Currently he is the writer and keeper of the art focused site Evil Tender Dot Com. He is included here for his views of structure, conferences, and as a professional reader.

***

Justin Sloan: Chris, you have worked as a reader in Hollywood and elsewhere, and done well in some contests, to include the Austin Film Festival's screenplay contest. As a reader, what have you learned about screenwriting that you may have not been aware of before?

Chris Jalufka: The one thing that years of reading unproduced scripts teaches you is in fact the greatest lesson a writer can learn—no matter what, this is all subjective. Getting good feedback doesn't mean anything. Bad feedback doesn't mean anything. Write what you want to write. Don't get hung up on the opinions of others, good or bad. Move forward, always.

I've had my bouts with trying to write what I thought others wanted. Living in Los Angeles I grew a new sensibility that was pure mainstream and blockbuster focused, which is not the way I write. The stories I'm attracted to tend to be introspective and character driven. When I look back and read what I wrote and re-wrote while in Los Angeles, it's not me. It's not the type of writing I want to spend time with.

The second lesson culled from years of reading is the need for clarity. Novels are allowed to be a slow burn. Scripts need to be lean. Get rid of clutter yet maintain depth of story and character. Easy enough, right?

Being a reader helps you develop your eye for what works and what doesn't and more importantly, helps you develop the language you need to get it across to the writer. As the reader that was always my main goal – what can I say to the writer to help them in their re-write? But also to let them know where I'm coming from so they can choose to listen to me or not. For example, I've read scripts for children's made-for-TV films, like what you'd see on the Disney Channel. That's not a genre I'm well versed in, so I'd make that clear in my notes. That's another lesson learned – to be able to put yourself in another writer's shoes and find what they were going for.

JS: What are your views on screenplay structure, and do you have any books on writing you would recommend?

CJ: Structure has always been my weak spot. I've read a handful of the popular 'how to' books and honestly what helped me the most are two things –

1. Strunk & White's *The Elements of Style*

2. Watching films I love (and some I don't) and writing out their structure.

The Elements of Style is a great book for basic grammar and tips on being succinct. Again, clarity is key.

Screenwriting books, I'm not so interested in. I'd rather sit with a notepad and watch *Wall Street* and track the structure of a film I admire. I'm of the thinking that every novel made is a 'how-to' on structure. Every film is there to teach.

I should have started with this, but going to film school you're fed those story and structure books and hey, look! Your teacher even wrote one! I'm skeptical of anyone who writes a 'how-to' book. Just my prejudice.

When the history of Hollywood is built on every production company and producer looking for the secret recipe for a successful film and they still haven't found a working formula, only the most basic of ideas are in those books.

JS: Did placing well in contests such as Austin, and attending the festival, help you as a writer?

CJ: It's a bit of an ego boost. It builds the confidence. Gets the blood hot. For a day or two every idea you have and word you write feels perfect. Brilliant. Then, a few days later, it fades.

Placing in contests didn't make me a better writer but the experience encourages you to look closer at the process. It can make you a more focused writer. I started to get picky about what I entered. Who are the judges? What have they done? Anything good? How relevant is this contest to the actual filmmaking world? What's the prize? At $50 plus an entry, I was looking for benefits to placing, and potentially winning.

Having read for contests I saw that some can be easy ways for a producer or company to make money on, and there are also those unknown variables. I read for one competition arranged by a producer who was looking for an 'urban romantic comedy.' He knew they were cheap to make and easy to sell. Nowhere in the contest description was that mentioned. If he had mentioned it all of those aspiring writers with vampire stories and period pieces wouldn't have entered.

I pretty much lost faith that contests are worth the entry fee, but I did find one benefit – I enjoyed the deadlines. Knowing that I had to have a final draft ready to send off on a certain date to enter Nicholl or Austin was a huge bonus. A calendar full of deadlines is exciting.

JS: Focusing on the Austin Film Festival and any other writing events you may have attended, where do you stand on these conferences now and why?

CJ: They're great social environments—I love to make new friends and talk about what I love, but these days unless I'm going as an audience member to watch new and exciting films, I'm not interested.

An environment like the Austin Film Festival is fun and has some great speakers and events but I realized they're not for me. Yeah, I'm an aspiring screenwriter, but what they offer isn't what I'm looking for. Not anymore. We don't all need the same type of encouragement.

As hobbies go, or as career aspirations go, screenwriting is a pretty bad call. If you wanted to play basketball professionally what would you do?

1. Buy a basketball.

2. Find a basketball court.

3. Play pickup games or join a local league.

4. Repeat steps 2 through 4.

5. When you're skills are up, try out for a professional team.

You may never become a professional basketball player but you would have played basketball and had all the joys and benefits of that experience. If you want to be a screenwriter you can write scripts, but the goal is not truly fulfilled until what you wrote is on a screen. You've just been dribbling.

There are plenty of crap movies made from crap scripts every year, so why follow anything you hear at a conference or read in a book telling you that if your script is crap it won't get made? You need the experience of making a crap film the way a basketball player needs the experience of getting shut down. Experience makes you stronger. Leaner.

So that's where I'm at. I just want to make stuff. Writing and then trying to coerce someone to read my script and hoping they'll like it enough to put money behind it and maybe get it made doesn't appeal to me anymore. Save money to shoot your film yourself. Hire a director, editor, and cameraman. Cast it. Be the producer.

If I were going to the Austin Film Festival again I'd bypass the badges and the talks, the private parties and events and just hang out at the bar of the Driskill Hotel. There you'll run into other writers but also directors and actors, editors and other filmmakers. It's one of the greatest experiences to just chat with someone over a beer about making movies and writing, getting inspired on a personal level. But that's what I need to get inspired. The casual spur of conversation.

There's a point, I think, where you graduate from screenwriting contests, writing panels, and all of that. After film school and working in Los Angeles and doing the festival route I felt I was hearing the same thing over and over.

JS: Do you continue to write? If so, does surrounding yourself with art fuel your creative process?

CJ: I write at least an hour a day, but usually more. I'm writing for my site and short stories. Scripts have lost their place on my priority list.

Having art stuffs around is just in the fabric of my life. I spend a lot of time seeking out new art – books, movies, posters, comics. Whatever. When I get 'stuck' I go on Tumblr or something like that and look for art that strikes me the right way, then spend hours going through artist galleries and just researching. The internet is a wonderful thing.

Actually my last visit to the Austin Film Festival is what inspired me to move away from being an aspiring screenwriter. It was an awesome time and I met a ton of great folks, but I realized if I wanted to see my scripts made I'd have to do it myself. Turning it into a career, making money at screenwriting, wasn't, or still isn't, my goal. I've always been a DIY type of person.

JS: Your site, EvilTender.com features some amazing artists. What brought you to focus more on visual artists and less on writers?

CJ: My first love was drawing. I'd gone to the Academy of Art in San Francisco since junior high, taking Saturday classes and summer school. My major there was printmaking, specializing in etching. I was doing a series of prints trying to tell stories, so I switched to film thinking it would be an easier way to combine storytelling and writing.

Evil Tender was always meant to be about working artists. There's a strange thing that happens when an artist attempts to make a living at their craft—the fine artist becomes an illustrator, the poet writes commercials. The guitarist plays in a wedding band. That idea of 'selling out' gets tossed around, which is hard to describe. If the concept of 'selling out' actually exists, earning 'legal tender' gets tainted as 'evil tender.' A silly play on words for the title of a site, but I'm stuck with it.

I have a ton of friends who have their own businesses or work freelance and I wanted to do interviews with those types of folk—skilled people who bypassed the traditional career routes to work for themselves. I love the spirit of it, the 'do it yourself' mentality of not waiting for someone to make your dreams come true.

The site has featured writers, actors, and musicians – basically anyone whose work has crossed my path that caught my fancy and got me excited. By going to more gallery events it was a natural progression from focusing on filmmakers to printmakers and illustrators.

JS: You are big on such conferences as Comic Con, Disney's D23 Expo, and we met at the Austin Film Festival. Let's start with what you get out of these conferences in general and why you keep returning.

CJ: It comes down to the people. I love people and I love when people make stuff, and love talking to people about the stuff they make. The world needs that. I need that. To see an artist hold a comic book in their hand that they drew is one of the most exciting feelings in the world.

At these conventions there are always huge corporations showing off their goods but also booths full of top notch toys, comics, books, and posters all with the folks who made them right there. How can that not be one of the greatest thrills in the world?

I love the tangibility of dreams at these events. You get to experience the results of dedicated artists. You can watch that movie or read that book. When you stop by a booth and see the posters made by an illustrator in person rather than as a .jpg on the computer, the importance of it gets heightened to the level of those that created the work.

At an event like Disney's D23 Expo you get to be immersed in the universe of Disney and watch films in progress, concept art and all of that. Disney artists are tough to talk to you in terms of reaching them, but it's still a great experience.

JS: I remember when we were at the D23 Expo, you talked about wanting to make a short film. Is that still something you see yourself doing? Do you have anything to share with our readers in that regard?

CJ: I was set to shoot an eight page short I wrote that was going to film in San Francisco. I had my wife on board with the idea and we saved the money to get the project going, but another project I was working on took priority.

Another love of mine is art, or specifically posters. Prints. It's always been something I've been drawn to and as a collector there were certain artists I wanted to see more work from. I wanted to see original work, images outside films and gig posters. Like with most creative outlets, personal work doesn't pay. A band will pay for posters to be made, so will a gallery or a film studio, but when it comes time to create work on a more personal level there's no one there to fund that, so an illustrator or printmaker won't turn down a paying gig to work for free even on their own idea. So I figured if I wanted to see original work I should step in and do what I could to make it happen. Why wait for someone else to do it? I'm impatient I guess.

I commissioned Swedish artist Kilian Eng to do a 24" x 36" poster of whatever the hell he wanted and I'd sell it through Evil Tender. So that's where the film fund went.

Shooting a short is always on the 'to do' list, but it keeps getting trumped by other projects. I like to have a few projects going on at the same time, each in a different stage of movement. Whichever one has the most traction gets my attention. I have a few posters commissioned and I'm putting together a group show at a gallery in San Francisco set for 2015.

A few of my scripts have turned into short stories and a few others I'm drawing up as comics. It's actually a good test to use the same narrative and translate it into short fiction or a comic book to see if the story still works or holds your interest.

JS: Congratulations, I can't wait to hear more about the showing. I love the art on your site, but I especially love reading your posts on Disneyland. Sorry, but I am a Disney boy through and through. What is it that draws you back to Disneyland? It may not be writing related, but can you share your secret have-fun-at-Disneyland recipe?

CJ: When Walt Disney set out to make Disneyland he cut no corners in making his dream come true. Viewed from every angle, it is a magic place. Every ride experience is beyond beautiful. The structures are works of art. For a park of that size to run that smoothly and be that dedicated to an ideal so innocent and true, man. It brings a tear to my eye.

Going to a place like Great America, you'll have a bummer of a time. The rides are good, but you can tell that no one cares about the park itself. Whoever runs it has no idea or passion for it. They treat it like a bunch of roller coasters in a parking lot and in turn the guests do.

My wife and I have come up with our own Disneyland routine. We're annual passholders and go about 2 – 3 times a year. We go in September and again some time close to the holidays, either November or December. Then we go again around May. All 'off season' times. I've never been during the summer.

We stay at the same hotel every time, the Best Western Park Place. It's right across the street and close to our favorite off-site restaurant, Tony Roma's. That's where we go for a late night beer and bowl of potato cheese soup. We've gotten to know the bartenders there, which is always fun.

Our routine is slowly changing now that we have our daughter, so we've added character breakfasts to our day. We've also started doing stuff that we'd never done, like the walking tours of the park.

With California Adventure getting bigger and having more stuff, plus beer carts, we've been spending a day there and a day at Disneyland. And if it's a hot day and you need some cooling off, Carthay Circle at California Adventure has amazing food and classic cocktails. Yeah, our trips have slowly turned into drinking and eating tours of the parks mixed in with rides dependent on our daughter's sleeping habits.

JS: I had a blast when I was able to go with you – it's always that much more fun when the person you are with truly appreciates the place. With this art and your love of writing, do you have a business plan? A five or ten year goal?

CJ: I'm a believer that if you do what you love opportunities will present themselves naturally. There's a common story I've heard from various artists, the details change but the general story points stay the same. An illustrator buddy of mine had jobs that ranged from educational textbooks to drink cups, but his goal had always been to work for Disney. When he wasn't doing paid work he created Disney inspired art. With each new film, he would do a design of the characters. Every holiday, a new piece with Mickey and friends in that theme. He posted on Flickr, Facebook, and Twitter, and over a few years his following grew. Still, no Disney job. Eventually a drawing he had done of Buzz Lightyear and Woody was posted on Twitter and Lee Unkrich, the director of Toy Story 3, saw it and loved it. He was contacted and soon enough was doing freelance work with Disney.

I probably have some of the details wrong, but the gist of the story is true. It's a story I've been told by artists repeatedly. They did what they loved because they wanted to, and eventually it just all came together.

I don't know if this would apply to writing, but it just might. Treat what you do like a job until it is a job.

So my business plan. I'm going to keep putting out posters until the money runs out and curating gallery shows until I'm no longer welcome.

With Evil Tender Dot Com having such a specific focus, like a niche inside of another niche, I get asked to write for various sites and projects. I get requests to interview artists for bigger sites, write bios for gallery shows, and cover art projects. All stuff I do anyway.

Okay, so my business plan is not money or career based, but I think about it this way – if I played golf that would cost a ton of money for clubs and course fees, or if I skied I would have to buy skis and a park pass or whatever. Instead of that I put my 'extra' money into going to gallery openings and doing what I can to put some good art out into the world. Not sure if that's a business plan or not, but I found my skill set is in the 'cheerleader' role, and I totally love it.

JS: Thank you so much for taking the time to speak with me, Chris. Do you have any words of wisdom or other

thoughts that maybe I forgot to ask about?

CJ: Making a career out of anything creative is a total bitch. There is no clear way to do it the same way it would be if you wanted to be a lawyer or a dentist.

It's up to each writer, each person, to sit down and pinpoint their true goal in life. I have an amazingly cool and beautiful wife and a daughter that just blows me away. Writing and art is a major part of who I am, but I got to the point where trying to make a living at it was taking the fun out of it and I realized I don't need to make a living at it to feel fulfilled and that's my true goal—to feel fulfilled.

Plus, I'm not going to move to Los Angeles again, where I believe you really need to be to make things happen. It's a long shot to make it as a screenwriter in LA and trying to do it outside of LA is the craziest super long shot in the history of long shots. Oh, that's another lesson learned and the one fact that people hate to face—the most important thing you can do to advance or even start your career as a screenwriter is to move to Los Angeles.

PART FOUR: SCREENWRITERS

First Steps for a Screenwriter

Everyone who has broken into the world of screenwriting seems to have taken different paths, and your path will likely be unique. Take a look at my interviews throughout this book and you will see that people find their success through getting involved in other creative projects, submitting to screenplay contests, fellowships, or posting on the Black List. The interviews included serve as resources for where to get started. You should also listen to the Scriptnotes podcast, led by Craig Mazin and John August, as well as the Austin Film Festival's On Story podcast. You can look to screenplay contests (the Academy Nicholl Fellowship, PAGE, Austin Film Festival, TrackingB), and buy a plethora of books on screenwriting. The problem with these are that a lot of screenplay contests out there seem to be in it for the money, and a lot of the books are written by people who are not working writers.

If you really must read a screenwriting book, pick up Syd Field's *Screenplay* so you will know what everyone else is talking about. I also recommend Pen Densham's *Riding the Alligator* because he tells his story of Hollywood, and at the back of his book he has summaries of what the other writing books say. If you read Densham then you save yourself the time of reading all the books he references, and can then focus on reading the ones that sound the most interesting. I recommend reading William Goldman's *Adventure in the Screen Trade* for wonderful lessons on how Hollywood works from the writer of *Butch Cassidy and the Sundance Kid* and

The Princess Bride. You also may want to read *Getting it Write: An Insider's Guide to a Screenwriting Career,* by Lee Zahavi Jessup. She is a screenwriting career coach, and goes into detail on many subjects related to a career in screenwriting. After reading my book, picking up Lee Jessup's would be a good place to go if you are an aspiring screenwriter. Likewise for aspiring television writers, Gray Jones recently self-published his book, *How To Break In To TV Writing: Insider Interviews.* His book includes advice and writer interviews in a way similar to my book (you should also listen to his podcast, the TVWritersPodcast.

To make it as a big-time screenwriter, you will want representation. What most people agree upon is that obtaining a referral from someone you know to an agent or manager is the best way to find representation and get meetings. But, as evidenced here and through many other people's stories, other routes are worth trying. For example, you might want to try screenplay contests.

Screenplay Contests

Many writers shake their heads at the idea of screenplay contests, because many of these contests are not able to actually help advance your career. However, there are some contests that can be a route to success. Read the front page of the contests for success stories, and you will find plenty. However, as I have learned by discussing contests with some of these winners, these success stories may not always be actual results from the contest.

Screenplay contests can be an ego boost if you do well, even in the smaller contests. You can receive cool awards for winning or placing well, rewards that might include comprehensive notes on your script, a bronze typewriter, large amounts of money, scholarships for story conferences, and many other wonderful goodies. Keep in mind that your real goal from doing well in a contest should be recognition so that you may find representation and one day sell your screenplay. Remember to focus on the fact that you are in this for your career, not simply to win contests.

Many contests offer resubmitting as an option. For an often-discounted price you can resubmit your screenplay after you have made changes, in hopes of earning a better score. But is this a good idea?

On the one hand, resubmission can certainly help. This is especially true if you know you will have the same reader. Contests are extremely subjective, so if you resubmit and a different reader judges your screenplay, you may end up getting a lower score than you did the first time, and be graded down for the exact points that the first reader gave you props for! Yes, this happened to me. Contact me if you want to know the name of the contest (which I will not be entering again).

Then there are contests, like BlueCat, which I believe promise to have one of your first two readers be the judge when you resubmit. The ScriptPipeline contest lets you resubmit for free. Not a bad deal! These are the contests you want to consider resubmitting to after checking with your writing group to make sure you made positive changes.

That is if you think these contests are worth submitting to in the first place. If you want more advice on which contests are worth entering, read the comments section of each contest on MovieBytes.com. If you have not been on the forum DoneDealPro.com, I recommend it. There are already many forum discussions on the contest you probably have questions about. And last, though not as much for feedback, Withoutabox.com is another useful resource for searching for contests, conferences, and film festivals. Chapter fifteen lays out the main screenwriting conferences and events worth attending. Talk to other writers or read the comments on Moviebytes.com or the forums on DoneDealPro, with an eye toward which contests actually help writing careers. The Academy Nicholl Fellowship, Austin Film Festival, PAGE, and TrackingB can legitimately help you.

Shoot a Film

One piece of advice I received early on was to, if you are studying screenwriting, go out there and shoot a short film or two. If you can attend a film festival or writing conference and say you have won screenplay contests and made a short film, your fellow attendees are going to see you in a better light. See the Jeremy Breslau interview in Part Two of this book regarding his experience with a short film, which he is leveraging toward his goal of making features. If you are able to shoot a feature now, go for it. I promise that, in shooting something of your own, you will learn a lot about writing, as well as everything else that goes into filmmaking.

It was with this in mind that I set out to create my first short film. Please allow me to share my experience with you, so you can see what I learned from the process and, I hope, feel motivated to go shoot your own short film.

To make *Into Abaddon*, I worked with a group called the North Bay Filmmakers, and specifically with North Bay Filmmaker member Noel Rosado. He was my Director of Photography (DP), but more than that, Noel was also largely responsible for pulling everyone together and figuring out casting and all that. Before you get started, go out there and buy the book How Not to Make a Short Film: Secrets from a Sundance Programmer. It may save you some time and money. I also found such books as Sidney Lumet's Making Movies and various storyboard books to be useful.

The script for *Into Abaddon* went through some substantial revisions as we worked on the actual shooting process. Thinking about how you will shoot a scene certainly makes you reconsider how other filmmakers wrote (and likely re-wrote) their own scenes. If you have a chance to direct a short, especially one you wrote, do it.

Storyboarding is tough work and time-intensive. I consider myself an artist (you can view some of my sketches on www.JustinMSloan.com), but for this ten-minute film I had to sketch about two-hundred potential camera shots and did not have time to go into an artistic level of detail. I did the stick figure version first, for thumbnails, working to keep it simple and trying to understand how I would "block" the scene. Then I went through and redrew these images on better quality paper, first in pencil and then in ink. In hindsight, I realize I did this storyboarding art much more like a comic book than a film. I have since been reading blogs by Emma Coats and others, and have taken several storyboard classes. I have learned a lot that I will be able to apply to my next storyboard. Furthermore, I now storyboard digitally, which saves a great deal of time. Samples of my final storyboard can be seen on the www.IntoAbaddon.com website.

Things go wrong. This is obvious, but it does not feel too good when it is your own film. In our film, only little problems arose. We accidently scheduled the shoot for Easter weekend and only realized it after we put down a deposit on our location. Then we found out daylight savings time was working against us. (How many of us hate this whole daylight savings time thing? Come on). Most of my short was meant to be filmed at night, but a couple weeks before we shot we had to move our clocks forward one hour and lose an hour of darkness. We survived, but we had little annoyances that arose from our small oversights. Our problems were relatively small, but they taught me to appreciate how many more unforeseen little annoyances could have arisen.

When we finished the film, I was ecstatic. After such an experience, we should always ask ourselves what lessons we learned that could be applied to future shorts.

Clarity is key. In screenwriting, everyone says to use subtext and avoid being too on the nose, but they rarely warn (and probably shouldn't have to) to avoid the extreme. Well, I imagine you might agree after watching *Into Abaddon* that I failed to make the back-story in my film obvious enough. Some folks may like this aspect of the short film, but others will find it frustrating and say it is too cryptic. I would like to move slightly more toward the middle in terms of overt storytelling for future films, and at least bring more people into the circle of comprehension.

Casting can be tough, but having the right actors is priceless. Our actors were amazing, as I am sure you will agree. They were frequently up until 4:30 a.m., and some had to go to work the next day at 5:00 a.m.! Yes, you should pay your actors. It shows you care, and that you appreciate their time and effort. My actors showed appreciation for the compensation they got. The key when casting is to schedule a lot of time, because half the people you have scheduled may not show up. Also, schedule the majority of your casting calls in the afternoon—most of our actors that did not show up were the ones we had scheduled for the morning. We used SFCasting.com, and maybe the talent pool from this website had something to do with our problems with absenteeism. I am not sure.

So what are my main takeaways from writing and directing my first short film, as it relates to writing? Keep your writing simple and try to avoid being cryptic. If I had to do it over again, I would lighten the mood and lighting up front, and overtly convey more of the information the story needed for the viewer to understand the beginning situation. For my first project, however, I am happy enough with *Into Abaddon* and plan on shooting many more short films.

Writing Resources: *Pixar's 22 Rules of Story, Analyzed*

As a writer, I love finding new resources to improve my writing. These come in the forms of videos of writer interviews from the Austin Film Festival, podcasts by top screenwriters (such as the Scriptnotes or Nerdist podcasts), and resources such as Stephan Bugaj's blog and his free e-book *Pixar's 22 Rules of Story, Analyzed.* Stephan worked at Pixar for twelve years, and was then the Creative Director in video games for some time before moving to LA to start a production company. This section's focus will be on Stephan's free e-book.

I do not want to spend too much time summarizing the book, since the point of the e-book is to expand on and explain a series of tweets by Emma Coats collectively titled "Pixar's 22 Rules of Storytelling." Emma was a story artist at Pixar when she tweeted these so-called rules, and she has gone on to present on the rules at such venues as the Austin Film Festival (where I first met her and heard about all of this). Her advice is digestible and incredibly valuable. If you have not checked out the many different ways her tweets have been compiled or discussed, I suggest a quick web search (and have included some of the links at the end of this section). Seeing as these posts went viral, I recommend at least being familiar with the so called "rules" before immersing yourself in an industry that will be referencing them.

Below are the "Pixar 22 Rules of Storytelling," as originally tweeted by Emma Coats:

#1: You admire a character for trying more than for their successes.

#2: You gotta keep in mind what's interesting to you as an

audience, not what's fun to do as a writer. They can be very different.

#3: Trying for theme is important, but you won't see what the story is actually about til you're at the end of it. Now rewrite.

#4: Once upon a time there was ___. Every day, ___. One day ___. Because of that, ___. Because of that, ___. Until finally ___.

#5: Simplify. Focus. Combine characters. Hop over detours. You'll feel like you're losing valuable stuff but it sets you free.

#6: What is your character good at, comfortable with? Throw the polar opposite at them. Challenge them. How do they deal?

#7: Come up with your ending before you figure out your middle. Seriously. Endings are hard, get yours working up front.

#8: Finish your story, let go even if it's not perfect. In an ideal world you have both, but move on. Do better next time.

#9: When you're stuck, make a list of what WOULDN'T happen next. Lots of times the material to get you unstuck will show up.

#10: Pull apart the stories you like. What you like in them is a part of you; you've got to recognize it before you can use it.

#11: Putting it on paper lets you start fixing it. If it stays in your head, a perfect idea, you'll never share it with anyone.

#12: Discount the 1st thing that comes to mind. And the 2nd, 3rd, 4th, 5th – get the obvious out of the way. Surprise yourself.

#13: Give your characters opinions. Passive/malleable might seem likable to you as you write, but it's poison to the audience.

#14: Why must you tell THIS story? What's the belief burning within you that your story feeds off of? That's the heart of it.

#15: If you were your character, in this situation, how would you feel? Honesty lends credibility to unbelievable situations.

#16: What are the stakes? Give us reason to root for the character. What happens if they don't succeed? Stack the odds against.

#17: No work is ever wasted. If it's not working, let go and move on – it'll come back around to be useful later.

#18: You have to know yourself: the difference between doing your best & fussing. Story is testing, not refining.

#19: Coincidences to get characters into trouble are great; coincidences to get them out of it are cheating.

#20: Exercise: take the building blocks of a movie you dislike. How d'you rearrange them into what you DO like?

#21: You gotta identify with your situation/characters, can't just write 'cool'. What would make YOU act that way?

#22: What's the essence of your story? Most economical telling of it? If you know that, you can build out from there.

I should note that the story rules are not actually official Pixar rules, more like observations from Emma's time at Pixar. That is why Stephan set out to write his analysis of the rules. One main point I should bring up, and one that I especially appreciated from his e-book, was in regards to rule # 4 ("Once upon a time there was ___. Every day, ___. One day ___. Because of that, ___. Because of that, ___. Until finally ___."). Stephan's analysis points out that, while this "story spine" is a wonderful tool, it is a tool for improv theater and too simple for our purposes. It lacks any mention of character, conflict, or escalating tension. Stephan recommends that writers look to other models as laid out by such authors as Syd Field, Robert McKee, Blake Snyder, Chris Vogler (a favorite of mine), John Truby, and Lew Hunter. Some of these authors were discussed in Part Three of this book.

There are many other great points that Stephan makes in his e-book, and I promise that you will either learn something about the craft of writing or be reminded of the points that make you an already great writer. To get a copy of the free e-book, follow the link I've included , and to learn more from Stephan, see my interview with him at the end of this section.

Other Links:

- http://dragonwritingprompts.blogspot.com/2013/03/pixars-22-rules-to-phenomenal.html
- http://imgur.com/a/MRfTb
- http://io9.com/5916970/the-22-rules-of-storytelling-according-to-pixar
- http://www.prdaily.com/Main/Articles/Pixars_22_rules_of_storytelling_14473.aspx#

Screenwriting Conferences

There are many useful events for aspiring and current screenwriters to attend. Even if you are writing video games, you should attend the big screenwriting and fiction conferences, as they all discuss craft, story structure, and character development in a way that is relevant across media. Often these conferences delve much deeper into the details of writing compared to panels on writing at the Game Developers Conference or other such video game related conferences, so video game writers should consider attending. Bring business cards with you, but keep them simple. Include your name, your contact information, and maybe the fact that you are a writer. Be ready to network like crazy and feel quite overwhelmed. And please, do not try to call it a night at 11:00 p.m. with the sad excuse that you are exhausted. If you do turn in before midnight, you will regret it the next day when you hear all the crazy stories of the fun you missed.

First of all, we should discuss your expectations regarding what you will gain from such events. Are they going to completely change your career after attending once or twice? Of course not. The question boils down to the point of attending. Is the value in what we learn from the presentations? Is it in the vertical networking (interacting with the pros) or the horizontal networking (interacting with peers)? Or do we gain the most from the motivation factor? All of these factors bring value to our lives and writing, but I would like to advise you to go into these conferences, retreats, and festivals with a goal in mind. Consider what it is you want from the event, and make sure you leave the event feeling like you did everything in your power to achieve that goal.

If you would like to attend other conferences that I have not included here, please consider the Screenwriters World Conference (also known as "Expo") and Comic-Con. Consider attending as many such conferences and events as possible, given whatever limitations on money and time you may have. Let us start with the Austin Film Festival as a case study.

The Austin Film Festival

The Austin Film Festival is often touted as the writers' film festival, and it is certainly worth attending if you have an interest in writing for film, television, or video games.

The presentations have so much to offer, especially for the novice. At my last Austin Film Festival, presentations included Craig Mazin discussing a character-driven approach to screenwriting, Robin Swicord discussing her approach on adapting *Memoirs of a Geisha* from novel to film, and John August on a panel about taking *Big Fish* from novel to screenplay to musical. There were many remarkable panels, with much to learn from. The most useful for me was a panel titled "Contemporary Comedy," which included the writers of such films as *Wedding Crashers* and *Meet the Parents*. We laughed while learning about how the authors outline their stories and how they approach writing for amazing actors like Vince Vaughn and Owen Wilson.

The presentations at events like the Austin Film Festival are worthwhile for even the more experienced writer. We can always be reminded of the fundamentals, or learn a new approach to writing that we have not considered. Regardless of your skill level, you will enjoy Terry Rossio's presentations on "The Rewrite" or "The Throw." I even saw Ashley Miller (*Thor, X-Men: First Class*) in the audience.

If you attend a festival with the goal of networking, the vertical versus horizontal networking question is worth considering. Do you spend your time waiting around for the professionals to walk by so you can run up and pitch them your idea? I hope not. On occasion these events will have agents and producers, and then maybe you can work your pitch into the conversation somehow. But if you are pitching to fellow writers, you may see a lot of eye-rolling. Instead walk up and say hi, tell them you appreciate their work, and then maybe move on. If you are in a city where you know the best bars and restaurants, you can offer to buy them a drink, or if they are already sitting they may ask you to join them. But you should think of interacting with fellow writers as baby steps—see them year after year, and keep saying hello. They are not going to offer to make your career right there, and more than likely, this all falls into the motivation factor.

But for horizontal, or peer-to-peer, networking, get those business cards ready and, in the case of the Austin Film Festival, prepare yourself to drink a lot of beers at the Driskill Hotel bar. Your peers are the folks that are still trying to make it. They may have some credits to their name, and they may not. You may find a writing partner, or if you are interested in acting, storyboarding, or another aspect of filmmaking, they may have a project that you can get involved in. Keep these networks alive, because they are the folks you will see over and over at these events; this is especially true at the Austin Film Festival, where many of the attendees return every year. In two years, when one of us has made it and is on the panels, these people from your networks are not going to suddenly stop talking to you—work on maintaining the relationships, and you may find that you are BFFs with someone on a panel.

Prepare yourself to attend these events with the purpose of horizontal networking. When you are listening to the 100th pitch that bores the crap out of you, or realize that the person across the table from you has never written a word in his or her life, keep smiling and be friendly anyway; because after everything these people will have learned from this festival or conference, you never know what they will accomplish in the next year—and, on a more good-person level, who cares whether someone is "impressive" yet? Just be friendly and have fun, and do not feel like you have to get something from everyone. Please, do not be that person. We can all smell it coming, and it stinks.

The motivation factor is perhaps the easiest to cater to. I watched Rian Johnson (*Looper, Brick*) narrated a Vince Gilligan (*Breaking Bad*) script in which Will Ferrell read for the lead. I talked with one of the guys who wrote *Thor and X-Men: First Class*, and sat at a table with Shane Black (*Lethal Weapon*). I even got to watch *Thelma and Louise* on the big screen, and listen to a Q&A with the writer, Callie Khouri. The Austin Film Festival is bound to motivate your writing for at least another year, because now you have seen the people who wrote your favorite films and you have heard their words of wisdom in person. Guess what? They are real people, and if they made it, so can we (with a lot of hard work and a whole lot of good fortune). Even if you do not have the discipline to finish multiple scripts, you can at least look back on these days next time you are watching *Lethal Weapon* and remember what a nice guy the screenwriter of the film was.

My advice is to prepare for each of these, but know what you are really hoping for. Do not be the fan who tries to follow the stars and get autographs (unless that is what you really need for the motivation to get that next script done.) Do not look at people for what you can get out of them, but know that you are all there to network, and work on keeping the relationships alive and healthy. Help each other out if you can. Try to attend some panels on subjects you are less knowledgeable about. That hung-over comedy guy may say something that greatly improves the thriller you have been working on, because you may already know everything about thrillers but have not considered your characters from this other perspective.

I will not discuss selling your script at these events, because I do not see that as the goal of such events. Many of the professional writers at the Austin Film Festival or Writers

Guild events talk down pitch fests, and so you must proceed with caution. To sell a script you need to have written a great script, and for that you need to sit down and write it, find a quality writing group, and workshop and revise like crazy. The Austin Film Festival does have a pitch event, however; and scripts have sold from this in the past, so who knows? I should specify that the Austin Film Festival's pitch event is not a traditional pitch fest, in that the goal here is to help writers improve their pitching skills. Traditional pitch fests present themselves as opportunities to sell your screenplay, but are often criticized for being attended by lower level studio assistants and interns, not the people who are actually able to greenlight your script. This does not apply to the Austin Film Festival's pitch event, as it does not claim to be such a sales event. For writing conferences and film festivals, simply be prepared to learn what you can from the panels, network like crazy, and come away super motivated. Most of all, have fun!

More information on the Austin Film Festival can be found in my interview in Annex B, along with more advice on how to approach the festival in Annex C.

The Writers Guild Foundation

Another great resource for events is the Writers Guild Foundation (WGF), located in LA. They host events year round, and a big spring event annually that I make sure to never miss. Like the Austin Film Festival, this is a great opportunity to network with other screenwriters and to hear what the professionals have to say.

To give you an example of what WGF has to offer, I will share some information about the event titled "From First Draft to Feature." I was lucky enough to be able to attend, and took away some great lessons and at least another year's worth of inspiration. While such lessons are often simply great reminders of the fundamentals, I hope they will be of value to you all.

There were many amazing speakers at this event, but in the interest of time I will focus on the panel I found most inspiring, which was of course led by the incredibly intelligent John August. If you do not yet know, John August always does a wonderful job leading panels and discussions. At this event, he and his panelists discussed notes they may receive on their screenplays, and how they interpret those notes. For example, the note "It felt long" may mean that the reader was bored with your screenplay, and we as writers need to figure out where they got bored and address that. "I wasn't sure what kind of movie it was trying to be" means you need to look at your screenplay and consider what movies it is most like, or what genre it falls under.

"I didn't connect with it emotionally" was a note that may bother some writers, but Linda Woolverton (*The Lion King, Beauty and the Beast*) said she does not often receive that note, because she starts with the emotions of the character. She looks at the characters' worst moments of their lives and their greatest moments of triumph, and goes from there. Oh yeah, and she was a badass—ask anyone who attended. As a father who enjoys watching Linda's movies with his daughter, I especially loved hearing her talk and I hope that I can one day stick up for my characters and choices the way she does. Linda shared a fun story about how "Be Our Guest" in *Beauty and the Beast* was originally sung to Belle's father, and it was an artist (she thinks) who spoke up and said "They're singing to the wrong person!" What a perfect moment in the development of a wonderful movie.

Another good note that came out of John August's panel was for screenwriters to keep an outline of the script, which I believe Linda Woolverton said she does so that as she receives useful notes she can go back and make changes to the outline before making the changes in the script. This allows her to see the overall picture in summary form before spending all that time working it into the script, and is certainly a practice I am going to ensure I stick to from now on.

John August made the comment that we should cut the entrances and exits of characters in order to keep the energy flowing. Scott Neustadter (500 *Days of Summer, The Fault in Our Stars*) said to remember that when you are adapting a story from a novel or other source material, make sure to give the readers of your script that same feeling and emotion that you felt when you first read the book. Another helpful comment from this panel was that, no matter what genre you are writing, you must create a mystery on the page. Keep your readers turning those pages. I believe it was Shane Black who said "Everything is a suspense thriller." This statement has been life-changing for me as a writer.

I would not be sharing the full excellence of this event if I left out the wonderful people who attended. I met some fellow writers and producers, and hope to be able to call more than one of them a friend. A special shout out to my fellow Veterans in Film and Television (VFT) member who I met there. The VFT is a great organization that you should check out.

I wish I could convey the full breadth of wisdom that was shared with us attendees, but instead I will leave it at that and encourage you to attend next year. I hope our brothers and sisters from Austin will participate again as well, and I look forward to seeing everyone there.

Disney's D23 Expo

I know, this may be an odd event to include here. But, as a die-hard Disney fan and wannabe animation screenwriter and storyartist, I have no choice. I had an amazing time at the 2013 D23 Expo. I saw original sketches and paintings for the layout of Disneyland, watched artists draw Dopey and other classic characters, saw a screening of Disney's *Planes*, and sat through many great panels. But what I want to discuss today is the usefulness of such events as Disney's D23 Expo for screenwriters or moviemakers in general.

I attended the event with my buddy Chris, who covered some of the panels on his blog, EvilTender.com. He did such a great job that I will not spend time going over the same material, and I hope that you will read his blog if you are interested in a detailed overview of the event.

What I will address today was whether I felt it was worth it to attend as a screenwriter. If you want the answer without reading to the end, I give you a resounding YES. But read on if you are interested in hearing why and how you should attend.

The whole point of an expo such as this seems to be to show off new movies and television shows to the fans. If you write movies related to the ones being shown at said expo, you are surrounded by the folks who may one day be flocking to your movies. These people singing along with the *Tangled* or *The Little Mermaid* songs in the row behind you while waiting for the screening of Planes to start are the same people who may be cheering when you bring *Care Bears: The Musical* to the screen in 2020.

Okay, maybe not exactly that scenario.

The point is that at events like Disney's D23 Expo you are able to see what excites your audience. We sat in the panel for *Frozen* and were blown away by (1) how passionate the Disney folks were about their upcoming film, and (2) how passionate the audience was. I swear I heard some sniffling and saw some moist eyes just listening to the panelists speak, and the applause and laughter seemed to be endless.

This experience is wonderful to get the creative juices flowing (during my attendance at least one new idea for a film popped into my head, and it's going to be a doozy, ladies and gentlemen). But even beyond the creative inspiration, Disney's D23 Expo is also useful as a means to remind us of the moments that must go into a script. Much like the story of how some of these films are made, we have to remember that scripts should be full of emotion. In *Frozen*, the silly character of Olaf can't just be there to make kids laugh (Ahem, Jar Jar Binks), but must have a real heartfelt connection to the characters and the plot. Disney appears to have succeeded in this way with Frozen, to the extent that I was pleasantly surprised and a bit choked up. As an aside, in one of my blog posts I questioned whether *Frozen* will rise to the level of quality of The Big Four in animation (*Beauty and the Beast, The Little Mermaid, Aladdin,* and *The Lion King*), and after seeing what Disney had in store for us, I was convinced. Then the movie came out and I enjoyed it thoroughly.

The D23 Expo surprised me with a couple of the panels, namely the *Frozen* panel and the Pixar "Doing our homework" panel. The lessons may be obvious to some, but are always worth reviewing. When doing research, Pixar and Disney stress that the world must be felt, tasted, touched, and all that jazz. You can't just write about Norway or Scotland by looking at pictures in the "National Geographic" or watching YouTube videos, because then you are simply conveying someone else's interpretation of that place. You need to convey your interpretation, your experiences, and all the emotions you felt as the wind swept over the cliffs to hit you in the face with that crisp Scottish air.

This can be applied in so many ways, not just when writing about international locations. It can be as simple as playing in the mud when researching for a film about bugs, or getting beneath a house to experience what it would be like to see it floating away, lifted by a bunch of balloons.

Not enough of us screenwriters really think about how our words will translate to the page, which is a mistake. Storyart is the loose art that is the first step toward directing the camera angles and actors/animated characters. Some (such as the people behind the Scriptnotes podcast) would argue it is best for a writer to focus on writing. But if you are a writer with artistic talent, or even if you don't have the artist within, I say it is extremely helpful to try to visualize your shots. Just use stick figures if you must, but study the shots and think about how you would view your movie. You may find repetitious scenes that you didn't see when simply imagining it in your head, or shots that just don't make sense. So if you see me posting about storyart from time to time on my blog about screenwriting, now you know my reasoning.

This was an area the D23 Expo was strong on: story and concept art. Combined with being inspired and learning about upcoming films and research techniques, my experience at the D23 Expo was an amazing one and I see this event and others of its ilk as useful for screenwriters. Of course, such screenwriter-focused film festivals as the Austin Film Festival are more directly related to a career in screenwriting, and not to be missed—but to supplement your life and live as a child for a couple of days, come with me to the D23 Expo in future years.

Part Four Next Steps

I want you to think about a short film you can make for a reasonable price, say $1,000, if that would work for you. Spend some time thinking about it, outlining it, and then go write it. When you are done, consider putting a crew together and getting your film made. Think about where you can find a crew, whether that is MeetUp.com, Craigslist, friends, or a local film school. If the idea of making a film is too much for you, find a screenplay and read it while you watch the movie that was based on that screenplay. This is perhaps the best way to learn how the page was interpreted onto the screen.

My Screenwriting Plan

1. What ideas can I turn into short films over the next year? Over the next five years?

2. What ideas can I turn into feature films over the next year? Over the next five years?

3. What resources can I use to put a crew together over the next year? Over the next five years?

4. How many screenplays can I read while watching the corresponding movie over the next year and what are they? Over the next five years?

Interview: Stephan Bugaj, to Pixar and Beyond

I am pleased to present my interview with Stephan Bugaj, who you have already heard about in the foreword and in my section about the *Pixar's 22 Rules of Story, Analyzed*. His advice is extremely applicable to my readers because of his experience with film, video games, and graphic novels.

Stephan Bugaj is a writer/filmmaker who most recently worked at Telltale Games as Creative Development Director, helping to develop narrative and visual storytelling for The Walking Dead season two, *The Wolf Among Us, Game of Thrones, Tales From The Borderlands*, and as-yet unreleased projects. Prior to that he co-developed and co-wrote two feature projects that were in-development at Pixar Animation Studios, which came about as a result of mentoring with various Pixar heads of story and directors starting in 2004.

Stephan's total of twelve years of experience at Pixar Animation Studios included stints in various production tech roles, which has given him extensive expertise in the overall animated feature production pipeline, from concept development through postproduction. On the live action side, Stephan has several features in development in the U.S., Europe and Asia

*****

Justin Sloan: Thank you for agreeing to share your thoughts and advice with my readers, Stephan. You have some great experience, the type which my readers are probably salivating over, to include your time at Pixar. What is next for you, and where do you see yourself in 5 to 10 years?

Stephan Bugaj: What's next is to move on to both more independent ventures, and more studio projects, like others in the industry. Locking myself to one company for years no longer seems like the best approach. What I'll give up in terms of paycheck certainty I'll get back in terms of ownership—both financial and artistic. More risk, but also more potential reward. Simple math.

So I am starting my own development and production companies, but will also do studio projects as a writer, director and producer. Just like idols such as Ridley Scott, David Fincher, Guillermo Del Toro, J.J. Abrams, Wes Anderson, John August, and so on. Most of them have multiple business entities up and running, and multiple projects going at any given time.

And given my transmedia experience, I'm not only looking at feature films (though I am putting a lot of effort in that direction), but also television, music videos, graphic novels, virtual reality, mobile, narrative gaming, augmented reality, theatrical robotics, and whatever other storytelling media and formats come along.

My ability to move across media and formats is fairly unique and owes to my unique path through the industry: I've worked with all of those media previously, involved with both creative and technical aspects. In my early career, I was a pioneer in both the commercial Internet and early VR, ending up at Bell Labs doing multimedia arts and technology R&D before moving on to artificial intelligence (I was very interested in narrative applications) at Webmind, and then animated filmmaking at Pixar.

But not every writer will be a natural fit in every medium or format. As long as you focus on great storytelling you'll find the ones that work for you.

JS: Having worked at Pixar and in video games, do you have any specific advice for aspiring writers on how to get a foot in the door at such high profile companies?

SB: Build your network, and learn to pitch in a room. Who

you know, and how well you're able to get people interested in what you know are both crucial. Given shifts in how the industry works, it's much rarer these days that shy, retiring writers get very far. You have to be out there winning friends and influencing people, as Dale Carnegie instructed all of us to do.

JS: Regarding your production company, are you accepting submissions, and if so how should my readers contact you?

SB: Except for submissions from friends, unrepresented writers need to sign release. You can request a release by emailing publisher@unpopcult.com. Sending material without a release will result in the material getting destroyed, unread. Readers who have representation can have their rep email or call me instead.

JS: Do you feel a writer should target any specific media of writing (novels, film, television, video games) to break into the writing career?

SB: Everyone in Hollywood tells writers to specialize, so I will tell you the same thing: specialize your genre. If you want to do animation, focus entirely on animation. If you want to do action, focus on action. "Range" – the ability to write multiple genres – used to be appreciated but is now seen by many as a weakness rather than a strength.

However, whatever your genre(s) make sure you choose to tell the kinds of stories that you are passionate about. Picking a genre because you think it's commercially viable rather than because you are passionate about it will show in your writing and pitching.

Specializing your medium is a little different. While there are still expectations that feature writers, TV writers, game writers and novelists are different breeds entirely, that view is changing due to economic necessity. More and more people and companies are launching franchises as books or graphic novels first, and then moving to film or TV. Companies are sprouting up that specialize in script-to-book adaptations written by the screenwriters themselves. The industry is starting to appreciate cross-medium writers, rather than regarding them with skepticism. But even with that change, people still expect samples or produced work in the medium you're pitching to – and legitimately so.

JS: I see you have a graphic novel Amar coming out shortly. Do you find yourself writing across genres or media? Was there ever a strategy to this, or did you just write what excited you?

SB: I haven't specialized either my genre or medium. This was motivated half by a desire to just write whatever excited me, and half by a strategy to ensure that I would have range – because while some in the industry may not appreciate it, I personally consider it a necessary aspect of being a creative professional.

But not specializing has hurt as much as it's helped and led to my decision to also become a creative executive and producer. Gatekeepers and buyers in the industry are often compartmentalized by medium and genre, and it is much harder for a non-specialist to "click" with representation and buyers.

That said, the skills I've gained by working broadly have served me well so far.

JS: Pulling back a moment, I wanted to ask you about your free eBook, *Pixar's 22 Rules of Story, Analyzed*. Anyone who has not read it should check it out. What motivated you to write this, and then to give it away? Was it part of a self-marketing strategy in any way?

SB: I was motivated to write it by the response to Emma Coats' original 22 Tweets, which were picked up by people all over the Internet and Media as some kind of "official Pixar rules for storytelling"—though Emma stated that wasn't the case.

I also felt that the hullaballoo around recirculating the Tweets alone was contributing to the Internet trend of accepting facile "sound bites" about complex subjects as deep and authoritative. I wanted to address both issues, and do so constructively by providing a deeper analysis of the content that would help aspiring writers rather than merely saying "Tweets are facile and non-authoritative".

The reasons for giving it away were also twofold: I wrote it while still at Pixar and it was much easier to be permitted to give it away than to sell it, and since I wanted exposure more than profit that was fine by me.

So yes, it was part of a self-marketing strategy. It also worked: several indie producers have contacted me about projects as a result of releasing the book.

It was nice to be able to both give back to the writing community – since I got a lot of help with my work over the years – while at the same time showing industry peers the depth of my story knowledge.

JS: What would be the main points you would emphasize for aspiring writers looking to put themselves out there and self-promote?

SB: Be nice about it. Aggressive self-promotion is annoying and counterproductive. *The Pixar 22* book was a gift to the community as much as it was a promotional item, and people understood that.

Also, think of it as networking more so than promotion. You're not a product, you're a person. Communication about you as a writer can't just be one-way. Don't just tell everyone about how great you are and tout your projects, actually listen and care about what they're interested in as well. That's not only polite, it's how you'll find your collaborators.

The first time you go to events like Austin Film Festival or Creative Screenwriting Expo, don't say anything: just observe how different people do things, and what works. You'll notice that the aggressive self-promoters who turn every conversation into a monologue about their projects and skills get ignored, whereas people who engage in two-way, topical conversations get business cards.

And while it's great to aim high, your network starts at the bottom. People get into the industry by working with smaller companies on smaller projects – not by finding a "clever" way to get the attention of Spielberg or the like. Assistants, junior agents, newly minted producers, directors who just made their first festival short – those kinds of people are much more useful contacts for most writers than anyone "important".

JS: I won't ask about your advice on craft, because the eBook does such a perfect job with that and my readers should have that next on their reading list. But what I would love to hear more about your thoughts on structure. Your eBook has some great lines on the topic, to include the following quote: "Since I am first and foremost a screenwriter I also call this my 'Zero Act Structure Theory,' because too many novices interpret structure teachings that focus on certain key moments to mean you can half-ass all the other moments. Wrong. Every moment needs to be interesting, and have a clear (to you) reason for being in the story—not just the 'important ones.' In other words, if you know something is filler so will the audience." Excellent advice. For an aspiring author, is there one structure you would advise they study, or one or two main books they start with? Does that answer stay the same whether you are talking video games, film, or novels?

SB: I have very mixed feelings about structure: I think people should learn it, but write-by-numbers leads to material that's not only bland but is actually not commercially viable. You still need to bring passion, talent and personality to your material.

That said, there are starting points that should be learned. If you're trying to write feature films, you will be expected to have read McKee's *Story*, Syd Field's *Screenplay*, and Blake Snyder's *Save the Cat*. Structural concepts from those books will come up in meetings, and you'll need to be able to respond knowledgeably. I personally also like Screenplay: Writing the Story by Russin & Downs, and Giulino's Screenwriting: *The Sequence Approach* because they provide different perspectives.

Novel writing is something I know less about. I like Weiland's books on outlining and structure, but there may be better books out there. I wouldn't consider myself an expert novelist: though I am working on a novel, I am drawing upon my dramatic writing knowledge more so than novel writing books I've read.

And there are no widely accepted "master theories" of writing video games. The structures are still evolving because story in video games is a very underdeveloped form. Very few people take game narrative seriously, so far, and that has hampered development of the craft. Games are also very diverse structurally, so it's a more complex problem in addition to being a less developed field. My advice to writers who want to work in games would be to study game design alongside dramatic writing – and play lots of games.

As for writing graphic novels and comics, which you didn't ask about but I'll answer anyway, I like Brian Michael Bendis' *Words For Pictures* – but honestly, I read it after I'd already written several comic specs. I did that by asking my pal B. Clay Moore to show me some of his scripts so I could see the format, and then adapting my experiences working with storyboard artists to comics writing.

Which brings me to an important point: none of those books

are going to be as helpful as building your network and having people a little more experienced than you are review your material and give you pointers (or not review your material and give you pointers).

I learned way more about writing and storytelling from writer friends – not just well-known friends like Michael Arndt, John August, Boaz Yakin, Mark Andrews, Steven de Souza and Philip Eisner – but also from many other lesser known peers.

JS: Thank you so much for your thoughts, Stephan. Before we sign off do you have any thoughts or advice for writers out there that maybe I forgot to ask about?

SB: Everyone already knows all the maxims about "writers write" and "be passionate about your material" and so on, so I'll add this one piece of advice too few writers get: if you want to make a living as a writer, you have to be professional about it.

There's a lot of talent in the world, so tolerance of flakes, jerks, prima donas, the aggressively clueless and other unprofessional behavior is on the rapid decline.

When agents, producers, publishers, etc. meet you, they're asking themselves two equally important questions: "can this writer deliver great material?" and "is this a person I could stand to work with?"

You need to inspire a "yes" answer to both questions, or you'll never make it.

Interview: Mark Simborg, First Stages of Progress

Screenwriters around the world gather anonymously (in most cases) to post their thoughts and questions on the DoneDealPro website. Rarely do they get the chance to interact face-to-face. However, if you wait for a full moon or the crossing of the suns, it can happen. And so it was that I was able to sit down to lunch with fellow Bay Area screenwriter Mark Simborg.

Mark has recently had some exciting opportunities present themselves in his television-writing career. Read on to hear his approach to getting discovered and sharing his experience with screenplay contests.

***

Justin Sloan: Thank you for taking your time to chat with me, Mark. Before we get into your scripts, I understand you have a manager, Kathy Muraviov, with The Muraviov Company. Did you have much success before signing with a manager?

Mark Simborg: I had actually just received my first option offer, for a romantic comedy. But it was a free option and in the end I told the producer no, and then about five months later, after signing with Kathy, he came back with a money-backed offer and Kathy handled the negotiations. Other than that, I did get some nice phone calls from producers for the same script.

JS: Wow, a good example of why we should not option our stuff for free. Do you also have an agent, or are you working to find an agent? Does your manager help you to find an agent, or do you feel it is unnecessary at this point in your career?

MS: Hmmm... Obviously I'd love to have an agent but I wouldn't call finding an agent my central focus right now. I feel like once I have a deal set to go I will probably be able to get an agent pretty easily, if one is needed. Kathy acts like an agent in many respects, especially since she handles contract negotiations. I do have a lot of balls in the air right now that could lead to me getting an agent. But if not, so be it. I'm not stressing out over it.

JS: Indeed, it does not seem you need one at the moment. I see you have done well in several contests. Have contests played much of a role in getting you to where you are? What is your view on contests, and would you recommend them for the novice to intermediate screenwriters?

MS: Sure, why not. They're a good way to see how you measure up. They can be fun, in terms of anticipating results, and they can sometimes act as a good motivator in terms of meeting deadlines. On the other hand, it's also very subjective and always comes down to the luck of the draw in terms of the reader(s) assigned to your script. So it is a bit like buying a lottery ticket. The ones that offer genuine industry exposure via a win or placement, or via the reading process (i.e., TrackingB, PAGE, Scriptapalooza, Nicholl) are the best, in my opinion.

JS: Over lunch you mentioned some pretty exciting moves in your screenwriting career. You have two projects with directors attached, a sitcom titled *The Land of A* with Claire Kilner (*How to Deal, The Wedding Date, and American Virgin*) and a feature dramedy titled *Strings* with Penelope Spheeris (*Wayne's World*). This is very exciting! What was the process for finding directors? Did you have much say in this, or was it mostly the work of your representation?

MS: Clare is actually now attached to my latest feature, as well—*Ray and Molly After the Apocalypse*. She's amazing. I got to meet her in LA the last time I was there. She's so energetic and truly passionate about her work. I actually initially got in touch with her via the social networking site Stage32.

Well, let me backtrack. I had already sent her a sitcom pilot of mine via her agent at Gersch. And then I happened to see that she was on Stage32 announcing her recent sale of her own pilot to NBC. So I decided to check in with her via Stage32 to see if she'd read my pilot; and sure enough, she had! She'd really liked it but was a little on the fence in terms of taking it on, so I pitched her the other sitcom pilot I had just finished, which I thought could be more up her alley, and about a week later she got back to me saying she loved it.

As for Penelope Spheeris, Kathy had already worked with her on a few other projects. She sent her my script Strings (which is actually now called *Finding Yesterday*) because it was something that was pretty obviously the kind of movie Penelope would make, and Penelope loved it. So...yeah. All of that was earlier this year, within the same month, I think. So it's been a good year!

JS: That is awesome. I am certainly a fan of *Wayne's World*, as I'm sure most of us are. Are you able to tell us anything about your project? Do your projects have any similarities to these directors' current or past projects?

MS: *Finding Yesterday* is about a highschooler who realizes his dad was the lead guitarist for an obscure but well-liked grunge band from the '90s, and makes it his mission to get the band back together in time to play at his 16th birthday party. I don't have anything else I would call similar. It was climbing the ranks at Lionsgate for a while but I think it's dropped out, and we have it out to a name talent via a production company. Still waiting to hear on that. And it's also been passed up the chain at another production company and we're still waiting to hear on that as well. That's what the business side of screenwriting is: waiting.

JS: Hey, some of us wait anxiously to be at that point, so congrats! In addition to these two feature films, you also have two sitcoms in development. How did you get these projects into development, and did you have a director or anyone else attached early on (such as with the projects above)?

MS: Those two scripts are the ones that have been kicking my ass lately! Well, one I'm thankfully finished with, at least for the time being, and it's now out to networks and agencies via the producer who optioned it. The other I'm still in heavy development but am just about there.

So the first one, Sycamore Park, I got to the production company that ended up taking it on via Kathy. I actually found myself in the incredibly odd situation of turning down a very nice option offer on it from another production company. Keep in mind this was the first pilot I'd ever written, so to get two offers on it, and from very reputable companies at that, with track records in TV, was, um...shocking. In the end, of course, we went with the company we thought was the best fit for it at the time.

The second one, *Divorced Is the New Awesome*, is being developed with a producer who'd already read a lot of my material and just happened to really connect with this. But I'd already had a pretty close working relationship with him.

The other pilot that Clare Kilner is attached to, *The Land of A*—which is kind of like a female-driven version of The Office — is still being circulated to production companies, but mainly in England.

JS: What is it about these projects that you would say got them the success they have had? Did they have something your earlier projects did not?

MS: Well like I said Sycamore Park was the first pilot I ever wrote. So... I don't know. Maybe that's a sign that TV is my bag, haha. It took me four years and seven features to get to one that producers were interested in taking on. I've actually written five pilots this year (and am now starting on a sixth). Two are in development and one has an established director attached. Never in my wildest imagination would I have thought that three of my first four TV projects would see some kind of action. Crazy! So...I don't know. I wish I could provide a better answer here. I have no earlier projects to compare them to.

JS: What is it about sitcoms that draws you to them? Would you say you enjoy writing them more than features? Do you think the market is more approachable with television, compared to features? Are you an avid television watcher?

MS: *The Office* was the show that inspired me to write my first TV spec about four years ago. My spec did really well in Scriptapalooza—finalist, I think. But then I had all these feature ideas I wanted to get on paper, so I got sucked back into features for a while.

Then this year—I don't know. It's like I vomited out a bunch of sitcom pilots. Oh, that was a bad metaphor to use. Um...I produced a bunch of pilots. Apparently I had a bunch of pent-up sitcom-pilot-writing in me and now it's spilling out.

If there's one thing I've learned over the last few months it's that sitcom pilot writing is damned hard. You have four acts to worry about (even though there are only two or three marked on the page) and each act has to have its own beginning, middle, and end. And every page has to be working on like four different levels. And, oh yeah, it also has to be totally hilarious, too. And set up the characters. And show why these characters and relationships can last 100 episodes. What else? At least a sitcom pilot is not required to take you into outer space.

As far as the market, I feel like I can really only speak to the comedy side of the industry with any authority. Comedy is my thing, unfortunately. And I say unfortunately because it's probably the most subjective of all the genres and hence one of the hardest, if not the hardest, to break into because the agencies and studios are looking to bank on name writers like Mindy Kaling. So I (or you) have to write something above and beyond what's circulating out there to get noticed. So in that sense, no, it's not more approachable or any easier than with features.

On the other hand, sitcoms are obviously a lot shorter. They take significantly less time to write. And execs have a much quicker turnaround time with them compared to features. So you get to know if something could happen with the project pretty quickly, and that's really nice.

Can't say if I like writing pilots more than features. They're so different and each has its own challenges in terms of writing and advantages and disadvantages in terms of the business and marketing side of things. I love and hate them both.

JS: Do you have any advice for those of us that are feature writers but would like to try our hand in television?

MS: RUN BACK TO FEATURES! Haha... No. Not at all. Actually the TV market appears to be opening up now a bit. But again I can only speak to the comedy side – to sitcoms. And I would refer you the paragraph above on what's required of a sitcom pilot. It's hard. But if it's fun for you to write them then, in the end, the fact that it's hard won't matter. You'll just do it and get better at it, and you'll be learning the hard stuff by doing it, and it won't feel much like work. You'll be learning the language by immersion, and that's the best and easiest way to learn anything.

JS: I read in one of your tweets that you are a George Saunders fan. He is one of my favorite short story authors as well. Do you feel literature has made you a better screenwriter? Have you attempted to write short stories or novels?

MS: I actually have an MFA in fiction from Sarah Lawrence College. It was a really good program, and I think the most important thing I learned from it was that I'm not cut out for fiction writing, haha. Actually what happened was I kept getting the, "Have you ever given screenwriting a thought?" question in response to my short stories. And my response was no. At least, not serious thought. I'd grown up in a pretty literary family. My parents—especially my mom—are voracious readers, and I'd always seen novels as kind of a higher medium than film, or certainly than TV. So I wanted to be a fiction writer. But then I kept getting that question. And I kept comparing my fiction writing to that of my classmates, and I could see a difference. I wasn't a very lyrical writer but I could write funny and make people laugh and my professors told me that my characters really popped off the page. But I wasn't lyrical. I suppose another way to look at it is that my classmates' writing had way more value on the page than it did on the screen, whereas my stuff seemed to have far less value on the page and more value as a blueprint for something that could be shot on camera.

Which somehow still didn't convince me I should do screenwriting...

So I wrote a book of short stories for my thesis at Sarah Lawrence. Nothing anyone should read. Seriously. It's tucked away into the Sarah Lawrence thesis project library and there it shall remain. Forever, I hope.

And then, not long after graduating Sarah Lawrence, I wrote a novel and thought, "Hey, this could make a great movie. I hope someone converts it to a screenplay some day." Then I thought, "Hey, why don't I just convert it myself." The resulting script was awful, but I fell in love with the form and it was goodbye fiction. That was six years ago.

JS: You have a lot to share with us, as demonstrated by your blog posts on the Virtual Pitchfest. I especially connected with your line, "Be delusional and naïve

because it'll give you the momentum you need for when the road truly gets steep and you're winded and thinking of quitting; suddenly you'll find you're still climbing the hill even though you've stopped peddling." I couldn't agree more. I have often prided myself on my ability to stay hopeful, or delusional. What would you advise to those teetering on the cliff of rationality?

MS: Thanks. The other side to that, which unfortunately I didn't have space to go into, is that I think it's important for us as screenwriters to stay young, to stay kids at heart, because that's what lets you tap into real creativity. If we let ourselves harden and dry up, then our creativity will harden and dry up with it. So...yeah. Stay hopeful. Stay delusional. Keep going. More than anything, just do it for the writing. Enjoy the process and don't let the ends distract you from the joy the means can provide you—which, I'm pretty sure, is an idea George Saunders would endorse.

JS: And on that inspirational note, thank you for your time today. For all of you in the Bay Area or elsewhere trying to make it as screenwriters, let's be encouraged by folks like Mark who are showing us that it can perhaps be done. At least starting out, we may not have to move to Los Angeles.

MS: Absolutely. Don't move to LA! At least, not until you have to. But I have to say LA is pretty cool. Any city that has a place that sells an $80 cup of coffee is great in my book.

Interview: Paul Zeidman, on the Black List

If you are not aware, let me fill you in on the Black List (blcklst.com). Of course, if you want some real details you can read the thousands of pages worth of forum discussion on DoneDealPro, but I will give the quick version, as follows: For $25 a month the Black List will host your script where, in theory, industry professionals can see it and make you famous. But the common belief is you need to receive some good scores before anyone will care that your script is on there. To do so, you should pay the Black List's experienced readers $50 to read and rate your script, and if they give it a good score, the Black List folks will promote your script around Hollywood via newsletters. It is best to pay for two reads, as there are a few stories out there of people receiving a three and an eight or nine on the same script. So you never know. But you have to pay for a read to get noticed.

Or do you?

Not according to what happened with Paul. But instead of me boring you further, let us ask him directly. I had the opportunity to interview Paul about his experience with the Black List and finding representation, about his writing process, his blog, and how makes this all happen. If you enjoy writer interviews, his blog has a series of interviews ongoing with script readers and consultants.

***

Justin Sloan: Thank you for agreeing to share your experience, Paul. I understand you recently posted a script on the Black List, and have had some positive first steps from this bold move. Can you tell us a bit more about that?

Paul Zeidman: This is actually a very long-winded answer. I originally posted my script Dreamship on the Black List back at the end of January. Two weeks later, I got an email saying a real live industry professional had downloaded it.

It was also around this time I decided to enter the script in the new Launchpad competition from Tracking Board (TB). The entry fee was reasonable, and I'd heard good things about TB. Apart from the Nicholl every couple of years I hardly ever submit to competitions, but I figured, "Why not?"

About a week later, I got an email from my industry professional. His name was Sean Butler. He was a manager, and wanted to talk over the phone about possibly working with me.

A few days later, we chatted. First about our respective backgrounds, then the script. He was very enthusiastic about it, and felt it was very reminiscent of kid-oriented adventure films from the '80s (like The Goonies). Even better, he thought it had enormous potential.

The deal was signed.

Next up was working with his assistant Chris on a rewrite. Scenes and characters were fleshed out, giving the story more depth. I didn't agree with all of his suggestions, but things moved along quite nicely.

Then right around Memorial Day weekend, I got an email from the Tracking Board people saying my script was one of 25 semifinalists. I can't begin to describe how much of a vindication this was for all the years of working on countless drafts of this and other scripts. Of course I daydreamed about making it to the finals or maybe even winning, but accepted that just being a semifinalist was still great.

JS: I read the script and have to say, I loved it. I can certainly see why someone would scoop it up. Where did you come up with the inspiration for this story? Does

having a daughter inspire the child in you? As a fellow writer of family scripts, I would like to know: when you are writing such a story are you cognizant of how it will play for children and adults?

PZ: Thanks for the kind words about the script. I always like to describe it as "Retro sci-fi steampunk pirates." The idea stemmed from an earlier script of mine about ghost pirates. Ironically, right after I completed that original first draft, Disney announced they were making a movie based on the Pirates of the Caribbean ride, which of course involved ghost pirates. So I changed my story so it was about ghost cowboys.

But I'd always loved this mental image of a ghostly pirate ship sailing above suburban rooftops. I tried to figure out how I could work that into a different story. Several tweaks and variations on that resulted in the script I have today. This is why you should hold on to earlier work.

My daughter isn't a huge influence in how or what I write. But in the end, I try to write material that not only I would want to see, but what maybe we would enjoy together. You want to write something that kids will get, but isn't too far over their heads, as well as smart enough for adults. Star Wars is still a good example of this.

JS: I see you write a blog, Maximum Z, on screenwriting, where you share your wisdom. What do you hope to get out of such a blog? I am often curious about such blogs (as I try to run one myself). Do you find it functions primarily as a way of keeping track of your thoughts? Networking? Do you find it distracts from that precious screenwriting time?

PZ: I see the blog as a kind of forum for me to try and give out helpful tips when it comes to screenwriting, and to chronicle my own personal progress for writing and how my career is developing. I never claim to be an expert—far from it—but there's always going to be somebody out there writing his or her first script, and maybe one or two of my posts can help him or her along.

I've connected with a lot of other screenwriters with similar experience, but don't know if any industry folks have checked it out. If they have, they're certainly not letting me know about it.

In terms of taking time away from actual writing, I'm lucky that it doesn't. My day job is being a traffic reporter on the radio, so my workday begins a little before 5AM (and no, I don't fly in the helicopter). Since there are a few sizable gaps of time between reports, I'll keep one eye on the roads while jotting down a few sentences for that day's post.

With my daughter's busy schedule, most of my writing is done while she's at soccer practice or Hebrew school. An hour and twenty minutes may not seem like a lot of time, but you'd be surprised how many pages you can crank out during it—especially if your outline is rock-solid and ready to go.

JS: It was great to meet your daughter, and you two seem to have a wonderful relationship. How do you have time to write, work, and raise a family?

PZ: I'm very lucky in that my daughter will occasionally ask me to tell her the story of one of my older scripts, or about the one I'm currently working on.

I'm also extremely fortunate to have a wife who's been very, very understanding and supportive of me going after a career in screenwriting. She's always the first one to read my outlines and pages, and gives some great feedback. A lot of times, we'll discuss a movie we've just seen from a writer's point of view (e.g. "Yeah, it was a great concept, but the characters just weren't that interesting.")

JS: What do you think of the contests out there? Is the Black List just another avenue? You have been writing quite a while, what made you decide to try out the Black List?

PZ: Like I mentioned earlier, I don't submit to a lot of contests. It really comes down to two factors: the script and the money. I may like the script I'm working on, but hardly ever feel it's ready to submit. And contrary to popular belief, working in radio isn't exactly a very high-paying job, and some of those contests are pretty expensive, so I have to be extra-choosy about which ones I do.

I think you should pick the ones that have the best chance of helping you build your career. I doubt anybody's writing just for the hell of it. I'd recommend the Nicholl (definitely), Tracking Board's Launchpad (naturally), TrackingB, PAGE, Just Effin Entertain Me, and maybe the BlueCat. Sure, there are a ton of others out there, but these are the ones that can really make a difference.

The Black List making themselves open to amateur submissions may be one of the biggest opportunities a writer could ask for, but you really have to make sure your script is absolutely bulletproof before sending it in. It's been a while since I've seen how many scripts they've received they started doing this, but it was hovering somewhere just above 9,000. You are literally going up against just about everybody else out there. This is where the adage applies: don't give 'em a reason to say no.

I decided to send my script in to the Black List because I thought it was ready. This thing had gone through a ton of drafts and rewrites based on feedback and notes from professional analysts, trusted colleagues, and a little gut instinct. I was already planning on submitting it to the Nicholl, and then they made the announcement about accepting submissions (mid-December, I think).

So after one more read-through, I sent it in. No regrets, and results far beyond what I could have imagined.

JS: How about LA? Do you feel you can live up here and pursue a career in screenwriting? Would you ever consider relocating?

PZ: I used to host a weekly online radio show where I'd talk to established writers and screenwriting gurus. One of the questions I'd ask, especially to those who didn't live in Los Angeles, was "Do you need to live in LA to make it as a screenwriter?" It was evenly split between "yes" and "no."

If you're fresh out of college, or at least still in your 20s, single, and have nothing really tying you down, then you should seriously consider taking the plunge. If relocating isn't an option, it'll be harder; but is still doable, thanks to this wondrous thing called "the Internet." You can email a script as a PDF, or conduct a meeting via Skype. You might not be able to network in person, but I've connected with a lot of people via Twitter, LinkedIn, Stage 32, and my blog. Geography is fast becoming the remaining insurmountable barrier.

I'm very lucky to live in San Francisco. We love it here, and really have no desire to relocate to LA. Hopefully once things get started for my career, it's not a big deal for me to fly down there.

PART FIVE: VIDEO GAME WRITERS

Writing for video games, as it relates to the work I have done, is very similar to writing for film. Furthermore, much of the advice given in books on fiction and screenwriting applies to writing in any medium. That being the case, much of the content of the previous sections applies to video game writing. To supplement this information, I have included specific advice on video game writing, as well as additional interviews.

If you would like to find another great discussion on craft in video games, read *The Ultimate Guide to Video Game Writing and Design,* by Flint Dille and John Zuur Platten. There are not many books on this topic, and Flint Dille and John Zuur Platten did a wonderful job in theirs. Another one I enjoyed when I was in the job hunt was *Writing for Video Games*, by Steve Ince. Both books will help you understand where you would fit within the game development process. They tend to approach their teaching from the stance that their readers already have some experience in writing. Whether you have such experience or not, having a concept of blocking and cinematic style will certainly help. Therefore, do not forget the great books on fiction and screenwriting, many of which contain lessons applicable to writing in many forms, including video games.

Prepare for a Job in Video Games

Allow me to take the risk of stating the obvious when I say that to write for video games, you must play (and enjoy playing) video games. I recently played some amazing video games that blew me away with their well-crafted storylines. Not all of them were new games, either. Where had I been? Why hadn't I played these games before? The answer is that I had been focused on my own writing; but that is no excuse.

Just like watching films will help you to better understand story, so will playing well done narrative-driven games. In fact, because what happens in games often feels as though it is happening directly to you, these games have the potential to evoke emotion even more efficiently than movies or books. I certainly will be spending more fun time in front of my PS3 or Xbox One in the near future; and since it is for work, I don't have to feel guilty about it. I give you permission to play games, as long as you are actively paying attention to the story and design.

With high quality storytelling becoming ubiquitous in video games today, many writers are bringing their skills to the gaming industry. See the interviews I have included, particularly the ones with Josh Rubin, who wrote on *Assassins Creed II, Destiny*, and now *Game of Thrones*, and Anthony Burch, who was the lead writer for *Borderlands 2*. Additional writers interviewed here who write or have written for video games include Jeremy Breslau, Matthew Ritter, and Allen Warner.

If you have ever wondered about video game writing as a career for you, I have a few recommendations. One of the first things I did in my quest for understanding video game writing was to play the games everyone told me were musts. The main ones I would recommend are:

- *The Walking Dead* (Telltale Games)
- *The Wolf Among Us* (Telltale Games)
- *Game of Thrones* (Telltale Games)
- *Tales from the Borderlands* (Telltale Games)
- *Heavy Rain* (Quantic Dream)
- *Beyond Two Souls* (Quantic Dream)
- *Last of Us* (Naughty Dog)
- *Uncharted* (Naughty Dog)
- *South Park: The Stick of Truth* (Obsidian Entertainment/ Ubisoft)
- *To the Moon* (Freebird Games)
- *Year Walk* (iOS game and companion app)
- *Dead Space* (EA)
- *Grand Theft Auto V* (Rockstar Games)
- *Red Dead Redemption* (Rockstar Games)
- *Mass Effect* (BioWare)
- *Bioshock* (Irrational Games)

Of course there are many other games worth playing. Once you've played the games I've listed, you will have no doubt about the quality of their writing. You see real emotion, you get into the minds of these characters and understand their wants and desires, and then—BOOM! It all gets yanked away (in some cases).

Find Jobs in Video Games

For those of us that grew up as nerds, writing video games sounds like a dream come true. Guess what? It is! I loved the classics such as *Zelda* on the SNES and Shining in the Darkness on the Sega, and do not get me started on that *Luna* game for the Sega CD. I was a nerd in a skater's body; sure I was out there snowboarding and kickboxing and having a blast, but even today my heart belongs to the games played in front of a screen.

I recently had the pleasure of visiting a friend at Electronic Arts who introduced me to a lead writer there, and I had the opportunity to learn that they hire most of their writers on a contract basis. The writers often work for several months, and usually remotely. This could be the perfect opportunity for folks who have a job or family but are determined and disciplined enough to put in the extra hours. Some game companies often seem to have postings for writer positions, but of course they generally want people with experience. So where does that leave people who don't have experience? The advice I received from someone at Disney Interactive was to go out there and make your own games, even RPGs/board games, to get yourself some experience and, if you are fortunate, some exposure. Or look around for folks creating simple app games and try to get on board. Or you may be fortunate enough to be hired for your skills writing screenplays or prose, as long as you have played games enough to be familiar with how to write for them.

If your goal is to write for games, you will want to consider attending the Game Developers Conference (GDC). This conference is quite expensive, but they have a reasonably priced "student price" for Friday-only attendees, and they have all sorts of seminars and boot camps on writing for video games. They also have a lot of networking and recruiting events, and the conference is worthwhile overall.

All writing workshops and seminars should help your video game writing. A lot of video game writing's success comes down to creating three-dimensional characters and intriguing dialogue, so you'll want to attend events that will help you hone these writing skills. Look up the San Francisco Writer's Conference, usually held in February; the Austin Film Festival, held in October; or Disney's D23 Expo, held every other year around August in Anaheim, CA. I have included information on these events in the pages that follow.

There are also all sorts of online learning tools out there, such as Skillshare.com and Coursera.com, and I'm sure there are some courses specific to this topic. One course that isn't exactly directed at writing for video games, but I found useful anyway, was Coursera's "Online Games: Literature, New Media, and Narrative." This class focused on The Lord of the Rings as an online game, a film, and a series of novels. It was a great way to look at how material is adapted across different media, and you should consider courses such as this to improve your writing and world knowledge.

If you are looking for a job in video games, remember you can always check with the various game companies out there. They will likely have positions listed on their websites. Also, go to Gamasutra.com. They have a link for job posts, as well as many other resources for us gamer nerds. But the best way to get a video-game-writing job, as seems to be the case with any job, is to network. Go to games conferences, hit up LinkedIn—whatever it takes, get in the inner circle and you have a much better chance of getting the job later on. Remember, though: if you land that interview and have no real skills to back it up then you have wasted their time and your time; so makes sure to focus on that craft.

Other Video Game Writing Links:

- 20 Video Games with Great Writing:

  http://www.authoralden.com/2012/09/20-video-games-with-great-writing-part.html

- An interview on narrative design for Company of Heroes:

  http://www.gamasutra.com/view/feature/129954/narrative_design_for_company_of_.php?print=1

- The online game magazine:

  http://www.gamasutra.com/view/feature/134542/a_practical_guide_to_game_writing.php?print=1

- "On Becoming a Game Writer," article on UbiBlog:

  http://blog.ubi.com/the-write-stuff-on-becoming-a-game-writer.

- Interview with Tom Bissell, co-writer of "Gears of War: Judgment":

  https://www.youtube.com/watch?v=4yGaNjtvhkI

- Great discussion on the Evolution of Game Writing:

  https://www.youtube.com/watch?v=94WHc1n4DPg

Video Game Conferences

The primary conference, as it relates to panels and networking for writers, is The GDC. There are certainly some other extremely well attended video game events, which include the E3 Expo in Los Angeles and PAX Prime in Seattle. However, these events are often more about seeing what games are coming out and getting a chance to play them early than they are about learning the craft. You should certainly attend, as it pays to know what is going on in your industry, and networking opportunities are plentiful; but know what you hope to get out of the event.

The Game Developers Conference

The GDC is held in San Francisco each spring, along with other GDC events in LA (an offshoot that used to be in Austin, TX), Europe, and China. The GDC seems to be the conference to go to if you want to break into video games. There are others, but this is the main one.

The conference is set up with sessions, tutorials, boot camps, and roundtable discussions, though as writers it seems our focus should be on the summits and boot camps. It is a five-day event, running from Monday through Friday (which is perfect for us with family responsibilities over the weekends). The price is a bit steep, but if you are able to afford the cost, it is worth attending. My colleague, Joshua Rubin (*Assassins Creed II, Game of Thrones*), has attended the last two years in a row and says it is a blast. For our purposes I will list several specific events from the 2015 schedule that often repeat from year to year and seem to be most valuable for aspiring video game writers.

1) **The Game Narrative Summit.** This portion of the

conference lasts two days and, per the website:

> "Covers interactive narrative in all its forms, from AAA blockbusters to indie games to mobile/social projects. The event features an all-star lineup of speakers from every corner of the discipline. Session content ranges from the advanced and theoretical to practical case studies and advocacy for writers, designers, producers, and others seeking to expand their understanding of game narrative. The Game Narrative Summit attracts attendees from all over the world with a passionate interest in the ongoing evolution of interactive storytelling as a driving force in the future of entertainment."

Seeing as the GDC's only other "writer event" (see below) is more basic, the Game Narrative Summit is probably the event to attend if you really want to meet writers in the industry. Some of the 2015 speakers include Tom Abernathy (Riot Games), Lev Chapelsky (Blidlight), Richard Dansky (Ubisoft/ Red Storm), Mary DeMarle (Eidos Montreal), and Susan O'Connor (Susan O'Connor Writing Studio). Each speaker's bio can be found on the GDC website.

2) Storytelling Fundamentals in a Day. This boot camp will be led by Evan Skolnick (Marvel and Lucasfilm writing veteran) at the 2015 GDC. Per the website, "This dynamic, engaging presentation on the fundamentals of story development is designed for everyone interested in improving the narrative quality of their games." While it looks like it will cover some interesting material, the site says it is pretty basic, so only attend this if you are at a basic storytelling level. However, I recommend you attend regardless, because Evan is a great guy worth meeting. His book, *Video Game Storytelling: What Every Developer Needs to Know about Narrative Techniques* is also a great read.

3) Level Design in a Day. Perhaps more relevant to experienced writers would be the "Level Design in a Day" boot camp, because even if you already know story, now you have to learn design. Speakers in 2015 share their thoughts on *The Last of Us* and *Diablo III*, among other games, with a focus on "ideation, implementation, and evolution of the craft." The good news is that you can probably attend both story and design classes, because they tend to be offered on different days.

4) Game Design Workshop. There is also a two-day design-focused workshop, which "will explore the day-to-day craft of game design through hands-on activities, group discussion, analysis, and critique," and include exercises and feedback.

The panels may change from year to year, but this list from the 2015 conference should give you an idea of what the GDC has to offer in addition to the floor and other networking events. If you want to walk around and mingle, you will certainly be able to do so. If you want to simply attend classes and meet people that way, while learning, that is also an option. Either way, I hope to see you there.

If you are a screenwriter for film, television, or video games, go out there and find a screenwriting event or conference that may interest you. Look up the themes, cost, admittance (if there is any), and whatever other information you may need in order to consider the value of attending said event. When you have decided on an event or two that you will commit to attending, make a list of what you need to do before you go. Perhaps this includes printing out some business cards, or having your 30-second elevator pitch of your story ready to share with other writers, agents, and managers. Make sure you buy your ticket early, as many of these events sell out fast.

Part Five Next Steps

This is the fun one. If you have not played the games mentioned at the beginning of this section, go play them. Look up whatever other games are out there that are known for story or interactivity, and play those as well. Put together a write-up on what you felt worked in these games, especially from a story point of view. If you have a blog, post this write-up on there! If not, consider starting a blog. Next, put this piece of writing in a folder on your computer labeled "Interviews" (or whatever works for you) and have it ready for when you interview at your favorite game company for a writer position. They will love that you can get into the details of what works for you in games. Lastly, consider contacting some of the writers of games that you have loved. Who knows, they may be open to sharing some advice.

My Video Game Plan

1. What story-driven video games will I commit to playing?

2. What is it about games I have loved in the past, and how do the above games relate?

3. What sort of video-game-related blog can I start, and what are some topics for posts I could include?

4. What video game writers can I contact and seek advice from?

Interview: Anthony Burch, Lead Writer of *Borderlands 2*

Perhaps you all have heard of a game called *Borderlands 2*? Of course you have, and if you are a writer, especially interested in video games, then you have also probably heard of Anthony Burch. He has done numerous interviews and Q&A sessions online, mostly focusing on the creation of *Borderlands 2*, as well his experience writing the game and running his webseries, "Hey Ash, Watcha Playin?" Therefore, and since the point of my book is more about the creative writing career and how to position yourself for such a career, I would like to focus my time with Anthony on his advice in regards to creative writing careers.

***

Justin Sloan: Anthony, thank you for agreeing to share your advice with us. I understand you were discovered by Gearbox because of your game critiques on Destructoid.com and your webseries "Hey Ash, Watcha Playin?" (or "HAWP"), which you did with your sister, who also played the voice of Tiny Tina. What a fun story! It worked out, but looking back do you think there is anything more you could have done to help you get the career?

Anthony Burch: I probably could have been less openly and hellishly negative about game developers I didn't like. I don't see UbiSoft chomping at the bit to hire me anytime soon, given how I used to (and to some extent still do) shit on the Assassin's Creed games all the time.

But yeah, the best thing I can recommend is just making your own thing that shows off your own personal style and passion. HAWP was a much better resume than anything I could fit onto a sheet of paper.

JS: Did you in any way have a plan back then, or did the Gearbox gig feel like a pretty big lottery win?

AB: There was definitely no plan. I was perfectly happy to keep being a games blogger for the rest of my life. It wasn't until I got offered the possibility of applying that I realized it might actually be my dream job.

JS: That must have been a pretty great feeling. In your interview with "The Totally Rad Show" you said there was a learning curve associated with starting a career in writing games. Would you have done anything differently in this regard? What would you advise others that want to be ready should their chance come?

AB: I would have tried to be less desperate to prove myself. I went out of my way to speak up in meetings where I didn't really need to, and I wrote scripts that were full of "JOKEZ!" that were designed more to show off that I could be funny and impressive than actually help the story in any tangible way. That kind of thing was born entirely out of nervousness.

JS: In that regard, do you have any favorite writers we should all follow or books on writing you enjoy?

AB: *Screenwriting 101* by FILM CRIT HULK is the single best book on writing I know of. After that, *Story* by Robert McKee and *On Writing* by Stephen King are pretty good. It's also worth reading *Save the Cat* by Blake Snyder, but only so you can speak the language of people who have read *Save the Cat* but don't actually know what legitimately makes stories work.

JS: I heard an interview recently with a co-writer of a video game where they guy said complex narratives in the style of Hollywood don't belong in games. Do you have any thoughts on this and how one should approach writing for a video game that would be different than writing short stories or screenplays?

AB: My personal style—and this is only coming from someone

who has written for AAA action games where the mechanics are the selling point—is for the gameplay to come first and for the story to support that gameplay and work around it as best it can. I don't like long cut scenes; I don't like huge info dumps. When it comes to working on the kind of video games I work on, brevity is the key.

JS: Now that you're in, is there anything different you would advise for people wanting to break in that you wouldn't have thought of before?

AB: Use Twine! Use game maker and RPG maker and make your own story-driven games that show your skills.

JS: In your talk "Dying is Funny, Comedy is Easy" (which was great, by the way), you said you just started writing for Destructoid, submitted, and they liked it. Does this opportunity to just throw oneself in there and find a following still exist? More so or less so than it did a few years ago (perhaps so many are doing it that, so it has become harder)?

AB: Less so than a few years ago, definitely—games-blogging has become a less and less reliable form of income for a multitude of reasons. That said, I think Destructoid itself still offers positions similar to the one I initially had—basically zero pay, but the chance to go to cool games shows and get exposed.

JS: Stepping back to HAWP, which is pretty freaking funny (thanks for that), where did this idea come from? So many people try to post videos online, but you were smart in that you had a video game theme. Do you see this as a viable route for others?

AB: I initially wanted to do a documentary on indie game devs, so I bought a sexy camera and figured I needed to shoot some test footage to figure out how to use it. I thought it would be funny to shoot my sister doing the Would You

Kindly speech from BioShock, and everything sorta moved from there.

But yeah, I see this as a completely viable route. Again, HAWP showed off my "skills" as a writer and my passion for video games, which were really important to Gearbox.

JS: Has HAWP changed now that both you and your sister have become big deals with the success of *Borderlands 2*? According to Wikipedia, it had almost 20 million views as of December 2013. Wow! If it has changed, how so?

AB: Nah, it hasn't really changed. We still half-ass it as much as ever. I mean, it's less horribly racist/classist/sexist now, hopefully, cause we've matured in the five or so years we've been doing it, but we don't look at it any differently.

JS: Anthony, thank you so much for sitting down with me to discuss your advice. Before we sign off, do you have any advice for learning to be funnier? Did you take improv classes, other classes, or read any great books on the subject?

AB: Grow up nerdy, weak, and with no other way to make people at school pay attention to you. That worked pretty well for me. Honestly, I dunno how you get funnier other than just watching and reading a lot of stuff that makes you laugh and trying to steal the fundamental ideas that made that thing funny (without stealing the jokes themselves).

Interview: Joshua Rubin, from *Assassins Creed II* to *Game of Thrones*

Joshua Rubin is a video game writer who has been nominated for WGA, BAFTA, and IAA awards for his writing on Ubisoft's *Assassins Creed II* (2009). He has been lead writer on projects for EA and Capcom, and spent a few years at Bungie helping to create *Destiny* (2014). He is currently working with Telltale Games on their upcoming adaptation of HBO's *Game of Thrones*. Joshua got his start as a writer focused on playwriting and novels, and he spent 10 years as a working screenwriter in Hollywood, where he was a finalist for the prestigious Nicholl Fellowship, the Motion Picture Academy's annual prize for best unproduced screenplay.

***

Justin Sloan: What is your advice for someone who is in the games industry and wants to keep the career going?

Joshua Rubin: There's no clear path, needless to say. I can only tell you my experience. My first gig in the video game industry was co-writing *Assassins Creed II*, which I got into through an old producer friend. It was one of those incredibly random and lucky phone calls that totally change your life. But I went back to my agent after this game had come out and made as much as *Avatar* that year, and asked what I could do with this credit. He said that it didn't mean anything. Nobody in Hollywood cared about video games. Of course, that was in 2009, I think that's less true now, with people like Gary Whitta, who wrote a *Walking Dead* episode for Telltale Games, and now is writing one of the new Star Wars movies.

But then, the *Assassins Creed II* script was nominated by the

WGA for its Best Game Writing of the year award, and I was invited to speak at a WGA panel. I felt like a total interloper, of course, among all these real game writers. I didn't know what I was doing there, but they took me in as one of their own. I ended up connecting with Amy Hennig, who was with Naughty Dog and had worked on the *Uncharted* series (she is now at EA doing a *Star Wars* game). She kind of took me under her wing. She was the one that said you have to go to GDC in San Francisco, if you want a video game career. She said just go, meet people, and network. I had no idea what that meant, but I went.

And unlike in Hollywood, my *AC2* credit was very meaningful there, and opened a lot of doors for me. But mostly, it was just meeting people, so many incredible conversations, I learned so much about game writing and design at GDC, and really began to see it as the art form of the future. And something I really wanted to learn and be involved in. Luckily, one of the people I met was a producer at Electronic Arts (EA), and they ended up hiring me to write the sequel to a big video game – that I'm not supposed to mention, and that, sadly, never came out. But this was totally because of GDC. I was based out of LA, but flew back and forth between LA and Redwoods City for the next year. It was an amazing experience.

JS: That is perfect proof of why everyone reading this with an interest in gaming should attend GDC. So how did you get your next gig?

JR: Through another GDC conversation! Actually, that very first night at GDC my friend and I walked into the bar at the W Hotel, which is the central networking spot, and is crowded 24/7 with developers and business people the whole week. It's, honestly, totally intimidating. I didn't even know how to start. But my friend urged me to just pick someone, anyone, and start talking, because you never know where it will lead to. And I did, I ended up talking to this guy who was a lead of localization at Capcom in Osaka, Japan. Not a guy that would ever be in any position to hire me, but we totally hit it off and ended up talking for an hour or so about video games. Well, two years later he called me out of the blue and said he had become a producer at Capcom and he had a project he was working on that he wanted to put me up for. And this came right when the EA project was ending, and my first kid was born. So, the timing was amazing. And the obvious advice there is: talk with everyone. Every connection in the industry is meaningful.

JS: That is a great story and very inspiring. It is interesting that the Austin Film Festival has a similar environment for networking at the Driskill Bar, but everyone there seems to be a writer and wants to tell you about their script.

JR: I would say that meeting writers is not going to help your career, because writers don't hire writers. They are your competition. That being said, there is a narrative track at GDC. They have a two or three day chunk focused entirely on seminars about narrative in games. The talks are fascinating, and you will meet writers, and the conversations are among the best. And you can also meet many people who are fascinated with writers and going there to meet writers to hire, for their projects.

But if you're looking for a gig, and you find yourself talking with a writer, bond for five minutes, and move on.

JS: Before we move on from GDC and the narrative track, would you advise more experienced writers to attend these seminars or are they targeted more for the beginner?

JR: I absolutely love those sessions. They get you thinking about the complexities of video game writing. Video game writing is so unique. I was a screenwriter for ten years, a novelist and playwright before that, but in video game writing I am learning every day. It's this brand new adventure, this brand new medium that nobody really understands. There are no rules for it. There are things that have worked, but nobody really knows why.

JS: Do you feel that the rules of screenwriting, such as story and character arcs, carry over to the world of video game writing?

JR: Absolutely. A video game needs many of the same things a screenplays needs: economy, scene structure, character motivation. You have to think about character motivation in any interactive game. What you, the Player, wants needs to be aligned with what you, the avatar on screen, wants. Pac Man is motivated to eat dots and stay away from Ghosts to stay alive, and so are you, to not have to waste another quarter. It's a perfect alignment.

Do you still have three act structure? I would say that the games that have it are better. Game design, by its nature, is very repetitive, so if there is no story to lead you on, the repetitive nature can be very boring. So I think of story in video games as the great hook. As a writer, I am influenced by the games I like, and my favorite game right now is *The Last of Us*. Like with its *Uncharted* series, Naughty Dog makes characters that I care about and want to spend time with, and that makes me play through the repetitive gameplay all the way to the end. Because I want to see what happens next! Honestly, there are very few other video games I've ever finished.

JS: When I was interviewing for my current writing job I asked a lot of people what I should play to prepare, and everyone said *The Last of Us*. Can you think of any other games that aspiring video game writers should be sure to play?

JR: When I started writing for video games, I realized there were 15 years of video games that I needed to catch up on. Some games I recommend include *Portal, Half Life 2,* and *Ico*.

Portal is a brilliant game. It is a mechanic that is all about intellectual challenge. It tells a story entirely through environment. (Spoiler alert) There is a point in the game where you find a crack in the wall, and if you go and investigate that crack you can get through and find that, outside of this antiseptic test environment you have been in, there is this hidden room with pipes and graffiti saying stuff like "it's a lie," and "they're trying to kill you." It was so unexpected, I felt like I had stumbled on something that even the designers didn't know was there. So that game is one of the first games to truly do environmental storytelling, which is an essential part of video games; the fact that you can explore in a way you can't do in film and that exploration can tell a story.

Half Life 2 was great because it was the first game that would have cut scenes play, and it would allow you to move around while the cut scene was playing. It had great immersive environmental storytelling, and cutscenes that allowed you to feel like you were part of it, to feel like you were in control.

Ico, and *Shadow of the Collussus* (sold as a pack on Amazon now), are two games by a Japanese video game maker who is one of the greats, Fumito Ueda. In *Ico* you play a little boy who goes to a castle and discover a little girl who has been kidnapped by a witch. You need to rescue her and lead her out of the castle. You can call for her, and she'll come to you, and you can reach out your hand for her to take. This simple mechanic gives you such a sense of connection with this girl you are trying to protect, and creates such an emotional bond over the course of the game. It's a great example of storytelling through game mechanic.

One of the biggest arguments I have is that writers need to be involved during the design of the game. Too often, writing and story are thrown over a finished game design like a blanket. But games like *Last of Us* and others I've mentioned show how much more emotionally involving games can be when writing and design are linked from the ground up.

JS: Do you have to understand design to be a writer?

JR: You can get a job in video games without any knowledge of design, but I think you will be wasting both your and their time. You don't have to have studied design, but you have to have played a lot of games to understand design.

There's a great story that's repeated a lot that explains why story is so important in video games, and the example uses *Tetris*. *Tetris* is a game with no story, it is about piling bricks. But what if you added a story to it about the holocaust? In this game, you are a German guard and your job is to get as many Jews into a cattle car as you can, every time you fill a line with Jews, that cattle car will go off. It is the same game, but with a totally different feeling when playing it. Even though it's the mechanic that drives the game, it is the story that puts meaning into the game.

JS: Wow, that's a powerful example. To avoid getting depressed, let me ask whether the game industry understands this need for design and writing to work so closely together?

JR: I think they are starting to, especially after the success of *The Last of US* and *The Walking Dead*. The audience is starved for story.

JS: I completely agree! One funny thing an agent said when pitching my book, was that only young people want to play video games. Is that true?

JR: The majority audience for video games is over thirty. Also, remind people who think this that video games, as an industry, make significantly more money than film and TV put together.

JS: And you have worked in Hollywood, so I am curious to know—why did you stick with video games instead of going back to Hollywood?

JR: I worked in Hollywood for ten years, I made a career of it. I made descent money and jobs every year, but never had a film on the screen. They all fell apart at one point or another. In video games, the first game I worked on went on to make a billion dollars. In Hollywood, as much as I loved the freedom of being able to work at home and set my own hours, I had always hoped to spend my free time between movies writing a novel, but instead, I spent all of my free time hustling for my next job. You never know how long that lump sum your paid will last, or when the next one will come. Video games is an industry where you have jobs with a steady paycheck. The whole idea that there is an industry where you can get a steady income as a writer is miraculous, and something I never even knew was an option coming up. But now, as a parent with two kids, having an office job as a writer is a gift.

Of course, I am fascinated too by the complexity of video game writing. The constant challenge of balancing player agency with giving an audience characters and catharsis, how do you balance those? I love that! And I love the steady paycheck.

JS: Thank you again for your time, Josh. As a final question, do you find time to work on other projects at home, such as novels and screenplays? What would you advise writers regarding this balance of time, especially those interested in video game writing?

JR: When I had one kid I structured it so I went to bed at ten and woke up at six, so I could write, but now with two kids, I find it a struggle to find time. However, I find that has less to do with having kids and a job, and more to do with having a PS4 and an Xbox at home. I would say that the greatest advice I can give to any writer is the advice that I need to take myself, which is to turn off the video games, Netflix, HBO, and internet. Instead get addicted to ice cream or something else that you can take to your desk and write.

If you want to be a writer, you have to write, and you have to read. Give yourself Friday and Saturday nights to play video games, but the rest of the time, focus on writing and reading.

Interview: Matthew Ritter, Comic Books and Indie Games

Matthew Ritter has published multiple graphic novels, as discussed below, and spent time in Hollywood. As his experience covers fiction, film, and video games, it made perfect sense to include an interview with Matt. He was kind enough to share his thoughts as follows.

His most recent graphic novel, *Retropunk* is a great read and I highly recommend it. Matt created this beautifully done work with co-writer James Surdez and artist Jhomar Sorian.

***

Justin Sloan: In your interview with BleedingCool.com, you have a touching story about your father reading to you and the superhero, "Super Zap," that you created. Obviously there is a strong connection between comics and video games, but when did you make that connection and decide you wanted to write for video games?

Matthew Ritter: That makes me sound incredibly altruistic and art-driven. My definition of art is stolen from Scott Mcloud, and I pretty much believe that anything a human does that isn't for survival of either themselves or their species is art.

I love comic books. I do, I love sequential artwork and the kind of stories that can be told there that can't be told anywhere else. That said, not that many people read them and they don't make a lot of money. So, why do I write for video games? Because it was the highest-paying writing job that I was able to get. Writing jobs are difficult to find, and most of them are technical or editing positions.

I've always been pulled more toward visual medias than prose. Like script writing, comics, video games.

JS: You created your own game through Kickstarter: *Boon Hill*. Have you worked on other games, and what

advice do you have for others who would like to make their own games? Where would they get started, as far as finding someone to help with the art and technical side and all that?

MR: Yes, I worked in the industry for some time, mostly as a pixel artist for random indie stuff. Tried to make a few of my own games before. It's hard, games take a lot of work. As for advice for making one's own game, I advise that you scope it down. However many levels you think you want to make, cut that in half, and now cut that into a quarter. How many assets? The same thing. Scope it down.

Games are hard to make, they take a lot of graphics, programming, assets, and so on. Big games are fun, they're amazing. Something that has 400+ hours of content is great. However, if it's your first game, make a 5-minute game. Make a *Snake* clone, or *Pacman*. Also, as for finding people on the technical side, if you can't pay them, you just have to look. Ask friends; go to community colleges and take the classes in computer science, and meet the people in those classes. But the easiest is to learn that stuff yourself. So what if you suck at it—program the game yourself and only you let yourself down. And if it's a tiny little crap game anyways, it should be doable by you.

Game jams are another great way to meet people. Find out when game jams are happening and try to get involved in the random teams that are mashing together.

JS: Your game looks impressive for sure, and that seems like some good advice. And now you are writing video games professionally. Congrats! Do you feel you did any one specific thing that positioned you to get this gig? What would be your advice to younger you who loves comics and may be just starting to think about posturing themselves for a career as a writer in games?

MR: Making games. You need to make games if you want to

make games. Work on games in any way you can. Learn how they work, play them, sure, but make them. Take courses, develop stuff. Even if you have no skill in coding, learn the basics of coding. Get your mind around how code works. The more you know about the inner workings of games, the more likely you are to be able to work with them without seeming like an idiot. Also, including games on your resume is always a great thing to do.

Everyone wants to make games, but actually make a game and you've made one.

JS: You mentioned when we spoke before that most game companies don't exactly hire writers. I have seen this to be true, where they either hire writers on a contract basis, or they have writer designers who do both writing and design. Do you know which game companies are at the top for pure writers, and what writers can do to make themselves valuable to the other companies?

MR: For pure writers? That's rare. I've seen Blizzard occasionally hire string writers (writers whose job it is to name all the crap that appears in their games) and I've seen Bioware hire writers specifically for quests, and Bunji and such hiring writers for pure writerness. The truth is, though, that just being a straight-up writer is hard in the video game industry. If you want to be noticed, just being a great writer is a rare thing to get you really looked at. Most game companies don't hire writers, because although we all act like we care...

We don't. As a whole, as people who consume games. Games are not narrative-driven. Games are design-driven. Gameplay-driven. Learn how to design games. Learn how to make gameplay elements further the narrative. That's the kind of stuff that is going to impress a game company. Oh, you can write a nice script, that's cool. But can you design a gameplay element and get it to work in a way that's both fun and oddly poignant? If so, that's impressive.

And on top of that, game design is often game programming. So, back to learning how to program or at least the basics of it. Because, you should.

However, I'm a terrible programmer, so eh.

JS: Looking back at your interview with BleedingCool.com and your discussion about Nova Phase (an 8-bit comic, for those of you who still have not looked it up), I am curious about your love of the old-school pixel art. Does this come from a passion for any specific old school games?

MR: How much outside reading about me have you done?!

JS: I'm a stalker. Focus.

MR: Old-school pixel art is beautiful. It's a new art form that came out of the technical limitations of the '80s. It's in many ways a descendent of the mosaic-style art.

It's symbolic, beautiful, and interesting. It's making something out of smaller things that don't look anything like that big thing but can be made to resemble it. It's about the way our brains see patterns that aren't really there. It's awesome.

And no, actually, while many old games have great art (such as *Seiken Densetsu 3, Phantasy Star*, or *Snatcher*), my passion for it comes from my intense love for the art style as its own art style. Nova Phase is an attempt to use the art style for something that isn't just another video game parody. It is its own thing. Using that art style.

JS: I am glad to hear it, and have not really thought of it as an art style. Perhaps you just made a new convert. On the subject of old games, what games from back in the day would you advise everyone play? I imagine there are a lot of aspiring writers for games who have only played modern games (due to when they were born), but surely they could become better educated and better people by playing *Secret of Mana* and other games of its ilk. Agree?

Others?

MR: Oh sure. There are lots of interesting narrative games from the past. *Snatcher* I already mentioned. *The Last Express*. Old IF (interactive fiction) games, which are still made a lot today as well. *Out of This World* is a great example of how to do narrative completely silently, with no actual dialog. There are sequences in the *Metroid* games that should be taught in classes on how to emotionally manipulate an audience. There's interesting and yet intriguing things, like how *Mario 3* is set up to look like a stage play. *Chrono Trigger* tells a solid, tight, and well-thought-out time travel story, and *Silent Hill* is scary. *Monkey Island* is funny. And there's much more out there. The truth is, though, I'd suggest people go back and play a lot of the "Top 50 Games" or "Top 20 Games" lists.

Learning what makes a fun game, and why certain games managed to make the impact they did while others (sometimes very deserving) did not. Also, finding out what you yourself really like about games. Going from one game to another like a ping-pong ball is fine, but figuring out what really entices you—what gameplay elements you find as filler and what ones actually fill you with joy—is worth doing.

JS: Let's move ahead to your most recent graphic novel, *Retropunk*. Where did the motivation for this come from, and what can you tell us about getting it out there? What does someone just starting to put a comic together have to look forward to?

MR: Uh, lots and lots of time effort and rejection? Artists of good quality are not likely to work for free. You need an artist if you can't draw to make your comic. Comics take forever, especially if the team is small. The readership probably won't be large, and it's frustrating. Everyone wants to make movies based on comics, but few people really pay attention to the comics themselves and for a smaller publisher or writer it's easy to just be overlooked.

Don't make a comic to get famous and have a movie deal. Make a comic because you have a story that can only be told in comic form.

JS: Like any art form. I agree and have stressed this point in my writing about staying focused on my blog. You can't compete if you aren't passionate, because so many others are. In addition to your own games and comics, I understand you had a stint in Hollywood, and of course studying screenwriting at Chapman. How much of all this ties together? And would you recommend aspiring video game writers attend film school, or look to video-game-specific programs such as Full Sail (or others)?

MR: I don't know much about the video-game-specific programs. I'd say just make sure to take a lot of classes in things that will teach you a good general knowledge about games. Or study that on your own. Hollywood is great if you can make it—they pay a lot of money. I could not make it there. So, overall I made very little money.

Really just write, however you can and whenever you can. I believe it was Steven King who said, if you write something, and sell it, and you get a check in the mail, and you pay the electric bill with that check, even just once? You are a professional writer, and no one can take that away from you once it has happened. He probably said it better though, if it was him.

JS: One conference I would like to attend, but unfortunately have not been able to, is Comic Con. I understand you have been three times now and that your publisher helped you to attend, including providing copies of your book for you to sell. Approaching this from two sides, how do you see aspiring writers benefiting from Comic Con, and how can people in your situation (published author) getting the best from Comic Con?

MR: Comic Con is a weird place. People don't really go to

Comic Con to buy comics or books. They go there to see all the cool cosplayers, or meet famous people, or attend talks, or hear cool stuff about TV shows.

As for getting the best out of Comic Con? If you go, be social. As social as you can. You don't need to hand your business card to everyone, but you should still meet as many people as possible. You never know who you might meet and that's the whole point of a con. Don't be afraid to be outgoing; and if you're selling something, try to engage people as they walk by. Don't expect them to come to you; a lot of them aren't there for you. Very few of them are, actually.

As for aspiring writers? I'd say it's the same benefit as any con. Meet people, get experiences you wouldn't otherwise. Attend talks about writing and things you think are interesting.

It's not a world changing experience, and shouldn't be viewed as such. Most people don't sell tons of books there, especially if they aren't already famous, but it can be interesting, fun, and definitely a great place to meet way more people in a few days than anywhere else on the planet.

JS: Thank you so much, Matt. Before we sign off, what other advice might you have for aspiring writers of video games, comics, or film? Any last pearls of wisdom that my questions failed to discover?

MR: Get a day job. Writing is hard to get paid for. Very few people do a good portion of the writing in most fields. Make a living somehow, and write on the side. Then, if you make it as a writer, switch over and focus as that. Sitting around waiting for your "big break" is just a great way to become a hobo or a leach on your family.

Also, don't steal any jobs that I would have gotten if you hadn't snaked it out from under me. I'll cry.

PART SIX: FICTION AND NON-FICTION

AUTHORS

The aspiring author may think they have the least to learn and the least amount of work to get his or her writing out into the world. They do not have to understand video game design, nor do they have to learn the format of screenplays or how to use screenwriting software such as Final Draft or Movie Magic. However, this line of thought can be misleading.

Among many authors I have talked to, both self-published and traditionally published, the people on the lower side are selling anywhere from five to sixty books a year. This is staggering, and disheartening for those of us that have great ambitions for our one or two books, each of which we spent years on. On the other hand, I have included an interview with Will Wight, the self-published author of the *Traveler's Gate* trilogy (a must-read, starting with *House of Blades*). Will Wight's books have done tremendously well, and he has proven that making it as a self-published author can be done.

There are all the easy answers to why he may have succeeded, from networking at conferences to tweeting (read the interview for more information), but the other authors may have done just as much or more work trying to get their work out there. The point I am trying to make here is that you can only do your best, and hope that it works out. Some simple observations ring true, such as a good cover and pricing both help, as does publishing multiple works, preferably in a series.

Whatever you do as an author, if it works, please share the

great news. I would be happy to discuss, and possibly include your interview in a future edition of this book.

Stay Engaged

Working full-time as an author is not the norm, but it can be an achievable goal. See Will Wight's interview for one example of someone who has made being an author into a full-time career. There are steps you can take to set yourself up, such as writing multiple books and making sure they are the best quality possible, but it really comes down to finding a readership, and often this seems to come when you do not expect it.

As you work toward this goal, make sure to stay engaged. You can easily sit at your computer all day writing, but I must encourage everyone to become engaged in their community as outlined below:

1) **Writing conferences.** In the Bay Area we have two big ones that I am a fan of, and those are the San Francisco Writers Conference (SFWC) and Litquake. While the SFWC is not cheap, it is amazing. The conference is set up with many educational and motivational presentations, networking events, and the opportunity to pitch agents. You may meet lifetime friends, and you may find a critique group, as I did. This was how the www.RedwoodsSociety.com blog came to life. If you get a chance to attend the 2014 SFWC, I highly recommend you go.

Litquake is more focused on the literary, which works for those of us out there who read *McSweeney's* or *The Doctor T.J. Eckleburg Review*. My first year there I went to a presentation by Irvine Welsh about his follow up novel to Trainspotting, and wrote a piece on it. I pitched my middle-grade novel in front of a group of fifty or so other authors and two agents, and went to panels on voice and finding an agent, among many other topics. To make the conference even more awesome, Litquake is not expensive. You can go to many of these events for free, and others for around $5 to $10. Why not go and at least meet some other authors? On the last Saturday (Litquake lasts over a week), there is a "Lit-Crawl" where authors read from their novels, short stories, and poetry at San Francisco bars. Tell me that does not sound fun.

More information on conferences is covered later in this section.

2) **Critique groups.** We discussed why you need a critique group under the "Find a Writing Group" section. The main point is that this is not all about workshopping your material. This is about forming bonds and setting deadlines as much as it is, of course, about workshopping your material. Find a critique group and congratulate each other as you each find new levels of success, and pull each other up if possible. Write blurbs for each other, share your experiences, and tell your group members about the upcoming writing conferences you're looking into. You need a critique group, and if you can't find one I advise you start your own. You can do so via online sites like www.MeetUp.com, or you can go to a writing class and meet other writers and ask them if they're interested in starting a group.

3) **Writing classes.** As I just mentioned above, writing classes can lead to meeting new members for a critique group. You may find a mentor, as the instructors sometimes stay engaged with their students after the class is over, or you may meet a classmate who has a lot to offer. In the Bay Area there are classes at the Writer's Salon, and having come from Washington, DC, I can highly recommend the Writers Center of Bethesda and the JHU nighttime and weekend MA in writing programs as well.

4) **Blogs.** That's right, if you haven't already started a writing blog, go out there and do it. Think of what you can share with the world, and put it into writing. RedwoodsSociety.com and BayAreaScreenwriters.com are two blogs of mine, the first of which I cofounded. Through both of these, I have learned a

lot by forcing myself to sit down and pump out blog posts. Blogs are also a great way for people to find you and to connect with other writers.

Commit to becoming more involved in your local writing community. Find some way to get yourself out there and engage.

Books on Writing Prose

In the world of prose writing, books on writing can be of tremendous help. Some are simply incredibly interesting. There are so many that are worth reading, and you should read all of them if you are able to while still committing enough of your time to writing. Each of us has our favorite books on fiction writing, and here are some of mine:

1. *Reading Like a Writer: A Guide for People Who Love Books and for Those Who Want to Write Them* (by Francine Prose): By far the most interesting one out there, I would point you to Reading Like a Writer because it has so many useful examples of wonderful prose.

2. *How Fiction Works* (by James Woods): If you want to master the incredibly valuable skill of "free indirect style," read *How Fiction Works*. While all of these books on fiction work for creative nonfiction, this one would be on my must read list.

3. *Self Editing for Fiction Writers* (by Renni Browne and Dave King): For anyone starting in prose writing who does not know how it should be done, this book will get you there. It covers formatting and the basics about conflict and point of view. If you show up to a writing group and don't know what point of view (POV) is, you need to go home and read this book.

4. *Creative Nonfiction: Researching and Crafting Stories of Real Life* (by Philip Gerard): A gem of a book for those of us interested in conveying real events through the written word. In many ways, what Gerard lays out here is applicable to both fiction and nonfiction writers.

5. *The Art of Fiction* (by John Gardner): If you are one of

those people who read fiction non-stop, you likely have a grasp of what makes a piece of fiction work, but you will not truly understand it until you have read *The Art of Fiction*. Furthermore, many prose writing class teachers reference this book, so if nothing else you should read it to sound knowledgeable.

My literary writing professor at JHU advised I read Robert McKee's *Story: Style, Structure, Substance, and the Principles of Screenwriting*, a book for screenwriters that very much focuses on structure (and a whole lot more). Other such books are discussed throughout this book, specifically in the section on story structure and in the interviews. These are worth reading as well, to see if they help you become a better writer. If they do not, at least you will have more knowledge of what some other people find useful.

Submit Your Work

Once you feel you have studied the craft of writing long enough and are ready to submit, publishing at least something can be the difference needed to keep you writing. Publishing is what makes you feel like a writer, and helps you feel justified when you tell others you are a writer. Therefore I would like to briefly discuss the process of submitting your work. In this section I will not go into the craft of writing, but simply discuss some of the advice I have received and lessons learned regarding publishing.

Tiered Submissions

One of my early workshop teachers told me to submit stories in tiers. For example, tier one would be the big-dogs. This refers to the agents for novels, and the literary magazines for short stories and poetry, that are much more competitive. You might as well try. For short fiction this may include *The New Yorker*, *The Atlantic*, *Tin House*, *Ganta*, *Ploughshares*, and *The Paris Review*.

Tier two publications would still be pretty tough to get into, but may be less impossible than the first tier ones. What I mean here is that I have known people to get into the tier twos, but no one I know has ever been published in a tier one publication, that I am aware of. Tier three is even more likely. For short fiction, my idea of tier two examples include *The Gettysburg Review*, *Zuotrope*, *Kenyan Review*, *Missouri Review*, and *The Iowa Review*. Tier three examples include the *Indiana Review*, *Mississippi Review*, *Virginia* Quarterly, and *The Colorado Review*.

Until you are awesome, finding a top agent or getting into any of these publications will be tough. If you have done so, that is terrific. Congrats! But what do we do when we really just want to be published, and the big named agents and publications aren't giving us the time of day?

Duotrope and Poets & Writers

Two places to look for small press publishers and literary publications, and to narrow your search by genre, word count, and other categories, are Duotrope (which now costs money, unfortunately) and *Poets & Writers* (which is still free, I believe). These resources work wonderfully for those writers out there writing fantasy or Sci-Fi, or other niche categories, such as military and nature. Even if you are writing literary fiction, you can find many publishers and literary publications through these resources.

Niche Publications

My first published short story was published by targeting a niche market. I was a Marine for five years and wrote a short story that was inspired by that time and had a military angle going for it, so when I heard of the veteran focused publication *O-Dark-Thirty*, I was sold. More information on the journal and The Veterans Writing Project (the non-profit that runs the journal) can be found in my upcoming book, *Veterans in Creative Careers*. As a bonus, if you email me at SloanArtist@gmail.com I will send you a PDF with Veteran writing program information and interviews. I also published my first poem in a niche collection, this time focused on nature. If you have a niche you can target, go for it. I promise, it isn't cheating.

Writing Conferences

Another useful source is writing conferences, where you get to actually meet the agents, publishers, and editors of literary publications. Conferences provide opportunities to chat with the industry pros and see what they are looking for. Furthermore, since they now know you they may be more likely to provide feedback after reviewing your work. As a warning, these conferences can be very overwhelming. Do not be ashamed of bringing a good book and hiding out in Starbucks for a break from the crowds.

Some prose writing conferences I have enjoyed include the San Francisco Writers Conference, Litquake, Association of Writers & Writing Programs, and Conversations and Connections, as discussed above.

Writer's Market Guides

The Writer's Digest offers a resource for getting published, titled *Writer's Market*. In addition to listing sources of publication, this tome offers advice for getting published, samples of query letters and all sorts of other helpful advice.

Self-Publishing

The question of whether to self-publish or not seems to be on the mind of many authors these days, as everyone seems to know someone who knows someone that has done well with self-publishing.

The pros are that you can make a much bigger percentage of the profits, if you sell a lot. You get to price your own book, and you get the final say on your cover and title. If you go with a traditional publisher, this may be decided for you, and you may find selling your e-book for $10 is much more difficult than selling it for $2.99. One downside to self-publishing is that you have to do a lot of the work. Also, as you can see by looking at the self-published books out there, a lot of people are horrible at picking their covers or knowing when their stories are ready. Then again, a lot of people do a wonderful job. The point is that there is no gatekeeper, so readers do not know what they are getting into, unless they hear about your book via word of mouth or just take the chance with you. It is indeed a tough call.

A word of caution: There are many books out there about self-publishing, and a lot of them are self-published and are not worth reading. Lucky for you, the San Francisco Writers Conference and many more such conferences offer quite a few sessions on self-publishing, and all sorts of websites offer advice. You can certainly do your homework on this topic before making a decision. I recommend you do so. One book I found useful was titled *Crush it with Kindle*, by John Tighe.

If you skipped Will Wight's interview in Part Two, go back and read it to get a sense for how he was successful with self-publishing. But if you definitely do not want to go that route, then maybe avoid the interview so you won't be persuaded.

Craigslist

Finally, I would like to discuss Craigslist and other such avenues. Maybe you have a short story or poem that you love and for some reason it is not getting published, but you are sure it is complete and you love it. You could always pop on Craigslist and find an up-and-coming publication that may love your story. They will not likely be a big deal, but that is not what matters at the moment. They may become important one day, it may just be that your story helps them shine, or it may just go on their website and no one reads it except the people who follow the link from your tweet. I say go for it, but only if you've tried the other avenues first. A lot of these publications are started by college kids, maybe MFAs, and they mean to go somewhere someday. If your story touches them, you may have just made a connection, and who knows where that can go.

Conclusion

My advice is to work through the tiers, search the sites and network at writing conferences, and if you just want it out there, give self-publishing or Craigslist a try. Whatever it takes to get you to keep writing and feel happy with yourself as a writer.

Let me know when you have some success, and I hope this helps.

Fiction and Non-Fiction Writing Conferences and Events

This list of fiction and non-fiction writing conferences is not meant to exclude other areas in the US or abroad, but to demonstrate the type of events you should be looking for in your area. And of course, if you want to travel to the San Francisco Bay Area to attend these events, I hope to see you there. As a quick note, I also included information on the San Francisco Writers Conference earlier in the section titled "Choose Your Writing Program."

San Francisco Writers Conference

Sure, the San Francisco Writers Conference is geared towards fiction writers, but writing is writing, so I'll go ahead and say it is relevant to you screenwriters and video game writers out there also reading this. Additionally, there were plenty of agents at the conference that deal with film rights for novels, and a couple that handle screenwriters. So if you have the option next year, I say go.

Too many screenwriters seem to get into writing because they think screenwriting can lead to riches, or that screenwriting is somehow easier than writing a book. As someone who has written several novels and more screenplays, I can tell you it is not (necessarily) easier to write a screenplay. Sure, it is shorter, and you don't have to spend all that narrative space getting into the characters' thoughts. But unless your goal is to shoot the film yourself, selling a screenplay is a lot harder than publishing a novel (and I am not even talking about self-publishing yet).

Did anyone not read R.L. Stine's *Goosebumps* as a child? If you raised your hand, go out there and read some to make up for your lost childhood. Are they literary masterpieces?

Certainly not. They are fun! As a matter of fact, when I asked Mr. Stine about whether he tries to include any sort of literary theme in his books, he looked at me like I was crazy and gave me a big fat "No." This experience with the author of Goosebumps has two lessons for me. The first is that going to the San Francisco Writers Conference means you get to listen to inspiring speakers and learn that some of the horror masters of our youth are darn funny comedians. Second: just write and have fun with it. If you want to write a horror story for children, who cares what the naysayers throw at you! Just go out there and write, and have fun doing it.

Pitch speed dating is exciting and everyone should try it, but does it really matter? Just like when I pitched at the Austin Film Festival, it was an educational experience. Everyone should try to pitch his or her stories in public, as it really makes you assess your material. Maybe try writing a pitch for your story before you write it? That is what the screenplay-writing world has taught me, and now I tend to wait to start outlining until I at least have the one- or two-sentence description (logline) down. The way pitch speed dating works at the San Francisco Writers Conference is you try to sit down with as many agents as you can for three minutes each. You tell them your story idea (I recommend taking about 1.5 minutes for this) and then they tell you if they would like to see it or not. I was able to pitch to five agents in our allotted time of a little less than one hour, but maybe you will be able to get in six. Good luck!

Litquake

Litquake is interesting in that it does not seem to follow a template from year to year. A large bonus of Litquake is that it is mostly free, though certain talks charge low fees of around twenty dollars. There are also no admissions requirements, aside from getting tickets before they run out. Themes of Litquake have a wide range, but generally include literary topics, including readings and panels with new authors. In the past they have had agent panels and author readings on the boats of Sausalito, and some years the event features panels on children's and young adult literature.

The Association of Writers and Writing Programs

The Association of Writers & Writing Programs (AWP) changes location every year, but will be in Minneapolis April 2015. It is advertised as the biggest literary conference in North America, and I believe the hype. When I attended the event in Chicago, I was quite overwhelmed. This conference invites such heavy hitters as Margaret Attwood and Tobias Wolff to attend as guest speakers, and tends to take up multiple hotels-worth of conference and meeting rooms. The conference seems to be strongly literary themed, and is coming to Los Angeles in 2016 and then Washington, D.C. in 2017. Though I will not be able to attend in 2015, Los Angeles is only a one-hour flight from where I currently reside, so I may be able to attend in 2016.

Women Writing in the Redwoods

A very valuable aspect of attending such events as those listed above is that you learn about other upcoming events, and one of those that I would like to share with you is the "Women Writing in the Redwoods" writing retreat, presented by the San Francisco Writers Conference. Let me tell you why the retreat looks worth attending:

1. Organized by Michael Larson and Elizabeth Pomada. These two agents are incredibly approachable, intelligent, and caring people. They put everything into the San Francisco Writers Conference to make it a wonderful time, and I am sure they will do the same with this writers' retreat.

2. One-on-one writing mentoring. As the flyer states, you will receive one-on-one mentoring from a professional faculty, with the aim of bringing your writing to publishable quality.

3. It is in the Santa Cruz Mountains. That should say it all.

Wouldn't you love to escape for three nights to write in such a picturesque environment, surrounded by other writers? I know I would. In fact, the retreat will take place at a Buddhist retreat center—wow!

I have included the details below, and would love to hear any feedback or stories you would like to share if you are able to attend. I am sure you will have an amazing time! Contact Elizabeth Pomada at SFWritersCon@aol.com, or Dale King at daleeking@att.net. For information on the San Francisco Writers Conference or sponsorship opportunities, please go to www.SFWriters.org.

***

If you are a prose writer, get online and find a writing event or conference that may interest you. Look up the themes, cost, admittance (if there is any), and whatever other information you may need in order to consider the value of attending said event. When you have decided on an event or two that you will commit to attending, make a list of what you need to do before you go. Perhaps this includes printing out some business cards, or having your 30-second elevator pitch of your book ready to share with other writers, agents, and publishers. Lastly, make sure you buy your ticket early, as a lot of these events sell out fast. If you are a screenwriter or aspiring video game writer who read this chapter for fun, write a short story or a novel, so you understand the different way authors approach prose, and then consider attending a fiction-focused writing conference.

Part Six Next Steps

Put together a list of publishers and agents you would like to submit your book to, whether you have written that book yet or not. Write down their contact information, name, and two or three books they have published similar to your own (these are known as "comparables"). If your manuscript is ready to submit, do so. If you are still working on it, read these other books that you wrote down as comparables, and consider these books when you are writing. Maybe write some short stories before you move on to novels, and submit them to literary magazines. This is a wonderful way to learn how to write and how to accept rejection before you move on to a longer piece.

My Fiction Plan

1. What agents can I submit my novels to?

2. What publishers can I submit my novels to?

3. If I want to self-publish, what resources are at my disposal?

4. What literary publications do I like enough to submit my short fiction and poetry to?

Interview: Kelly Ann Jacobson, First Novels

While studying at the Johns Hopkins University, I had the pleasure of meeting many soon-to-be-published authors. They were hungry for the craft and ready to show the world what they could create with mere words on the page. One of my classmates, an especially ambitious young writer named Kelly Ann Jacobson, recently published her first novels and agreed to share her thoughts on writing. You can find more information on Kelly and her novel at her website, www.KellyAnnJacobson.com.

***

Justin Sloan: Thank you for agreeing to speak with me Kelly. I am sure you are excited to have published your first novel, *Cairo in White*, and from what I have read so far, it is full of beautiful description and issues of sexuality that I imagine play a very interesting role in the Egyptian culture. What drew you to this particular story in this particular location?

Kelly Ann Jacobson: Thank you for having me, and for your kind words about my book! I am beyond thrilled to have finally published my first novel, but it did take me about six years to write (and edit, and rewrite again, and edit again). I started *Cairo in White* during my sophomore year at George Washington University, when I was dating an Egyptian who, when asked about gays in Egypt, claimed that there weren't any. As a Women's Studies major, I was appalled. So I wrote the first chapter of Cairo as a short story about one woman's struggle within the confines of her Egyptian struggle, and the character just stayed with me.

JS: Do you find a theme or common thread among the

stories you write? Is there one major aspect of writing that brings you back to it over and over again?

KAJ: My dad always jokes that I write "slit your wrists" poems and stories, which is, at times, an accurate description. Over the past few years I've written enough stories about the deaths of family members to fill a whole book (I literally do have a book of these, which is with a publisher right now, so we'll see if it goes anywhere). It's weird, because I'm usually the happiest, bubbliest person in any room, but my family is the most important thing to me in the world and I think the idea of losing them terrifies me. Writers always say to write what scares you the most, so that's what I do. I pour it all into my stories.

Besides death, in terms of threads, I find myself going back to Pennsylvania a lot for the settings of my short stories and poems. It's weird, because I couldn't get out of there soon enough, but now that I live in Washington, DC, there are parts of Pennsylvania I miss.

JS: I feel the same way about DC, so I know what you mean. I understand you have a second novel about to be published. Can you explain to our audience what it feels like to have, not one, but two novels hitting the market? Do you have any war stories from the publishing process that you would be willing to share?

KAJ: It feels bizarre. I actually wrote the first draft of *Dreamweaver Road* in about ten days this past summer as a way of "taking a break" from the millionth revision of *Cairo in White*, and weirdly, one publisher loved *Dreamweaver* but asked for a longer novel instead (that's Musa Publishing, which is publishing *Cairo*), and the second publisher sent me a contract for *Dreamweaver* right away. The book is more of a novelette, very short, and it's a Young Adult fantasy story with witches and dragons.

In terms of war stories, I think the hardest part of being a writer is the waiting. Not only do you have to take forever to write the book, but once it's done, you have to wait for someone to read it and accept it. Then, once they accept it, you think all of the waiting is over, but in fact, it's just begun. They might tell you they're aiming for January (or not give you a date at all), and when the middle of January comes, you're still doing your first round of edits. Patience, needless to say, is not one of my strong points.

JS: Do you workshop with a writing group? Beta readers?

KAJ: I just graduated from Hopkins in December, so I spent a lot of time in workshops over the past two and a half years. After graduation, a wonderful friend of mine, Sheryl Hotlen Rivett, asked me to start a writing group with her, so we did. I tend to actually not be much of a workshopper or group writer at all; I prefer writing on my own without feedback until the entire thing is done (or never, until I send it to a publisher); but I love my group of writer friends and I trust them, so that makes it fun.

JS: Did you ever consider the self-publishing route in this process?

KAJ: When I first started querying this novel back in undergrad, I got a lot of positive responses from big deal agents who loved the story, but thought the writing was just not there yet. So I knew that eventually, after spending a lot of time querying agents and publishers, I would find a home for the book. I think with self-publishing, you need to be able to edit your own work or have someone else edit it, which involves more time and money upfront that I didn't have. You have to be able to make your own cover art or have someone do it, which again, requires more time and money. But, for example, I'm editing a book of essays on online dating called Answers I'll Accept, and I think I'm going to go the self-publishing route with that project. I'm the one editing other people's work, my dad took the cover photo, and I now have the connections I need to hold a book launch, get blurbs, etc.

etc. As long as a writer is willing to market the hell out of their work and hire an editor, I think self-publishing works.

JS: How did you find your editor and what made you go with this choice?

KAJ: I tried try to query a bunch of agents back in undergrad, and got many positive responses. When I did the same thing last year, with a bunch of publications and a Hopkins degree, most agents didn't even bother to respond to my email. I think that was enough of a hint about where print publishing is going for me to decide to stop querying, go online, and find myself an e-book publisher, which is how I found Musa. I absolutely love their system, it's all online, so you can see who has your manuscript and what part of the process it's in. You get an editor, and a line editor, and a cover artist, and all kinds of wonderful help.

JS: I will be among those soon to check out Musa. Are you a fan of writing conferences, and if so, do you have any favorites?

KAJ: As a poor college student for the past six years, I haven't gotten much of a chance to go to that many writing conferences. I did go to AWP last year in Boston, and I'm headed to Seattle this coming week to table at this year's AWP for the magazine I edit for, *Outside In Literary & Travel Magazine*. I know a lot of people find AWP overwhelming, and it is, but I love the feeling of being surrounded by so many eager writers, editors, and agents who are all looking for the same thing.

JS: I just attended the San Francisco Writers Conference and had a wonderful time, as I am sure you will at AWP. I wish I was going, as I hear Tobias Wolff will be there. How much of your real life do you tend to put into your stories? Are any of your characters based on people you know (you don't have to say who they actually are)?

KAJ: I pull a lot of details from my real life, but almost no actual characters or storylines. So for example, Aisha goes to a lot of the same places I went to in Cairo, but none of the situations that happen to her at those places happened to me. The general feeling of her experience is the same, and if you look closely, she's eating the same things I ate and buying the same things I bought; but I am not her. The same holds true for Zahra. I pulled the description for her basement "apartment" from an actual basement I lived in in Fairfax, and I really did eat soup with fish heads floating in it; but nothing that actually happens to her happened to me. I write and edit poetry, so I think in general I strive to write my prose as lyrically and "poetically" as possible with as many great details as possible, but if I try to write a personal storyline I'm too close to, it fails.

JS: I notice that you made sure to acknowledge your professors from the Johns Hopkins MA in writing program. What are your takeaways from such a program, and would you recommend an MA or MFA in creative writing to other aspiring authors?

KAJ: Yes, I would definitely recommend it. I loved my time at Hopkins, and even though it took me two and a half years, I felt like it was over too soon. Even if you think you're the best writer in the world (which, I hate to break it to you, you're probably not) there's always something to learn from both your professors and your fellow students in an MA or MFA program. Ed Perlman, who teaches Sentence Power, literally changed the way I write my prose. After his class last spring I printed *Cairo*, opened a blank page, and started again. It was humbling, but it was necessary. And I did it with the support of David Everett (the director of the program), Mark Farrington (a fiction professor and advisor, who I basically stalked by taking a class with him almost every semester), and all of my other wonderful teachers and fellow students.

JS: I went through the same wonderful experience with Ed Perlman, and completely agree. Without him and the

other professors' help, I would be lost. Are you done with education now, or what do you see as coming along next for you?

KAJ: I actually applied to PhD programs, though some of them take about two people a year, so we'll see. My goal is to be a professor, so, in general, the more education the better. I also just love learning, and I feel lost if I'm not in school.

JS: Do you have a day job, or are you focused 100% on the writing? If you have not made the leap yet, do you hope to one day go all in on the writing?

KAJ: I would love to write full-time, but honestly, writing doesn't pay. So yes, I have a full-time job as an events coordinator at a city club, which can be a struggle because of the stress but flexible in its own way because I have the best boss in the world. Hopefully after I get a teaching job and put a few more novels out, writing can become my full-time gig.

JS: I hope that will become a reality. Thank you for sharing your experience with us, Kelly. Before we sign off, do you have any last bits of advice for those of us out there anxiously waiting to follow your lead and get our first novels published?

KAJ: Thank you so much, these were wonderful questions! My biggest advice is pretty much what everyone else says: write every day. Even if it's just a quote someone said on the metro, or a line for a poem, or a plot idea, write it down. It's not about getting the volume on paper, it's about keeping your mind focused on writing at all times. As a writer with a full-time job who until this point was in school and also teaching writing to kids on the side, I almost never got to actually spend several hours sitting down and writing. We multitasking writers need to learn how to write anywhere and everywhere, and how to keep our minds on writing even when we're not actually sitting down to write.

Interview: Laura Hedgecock, *Memories of Me*

Laura Hedgecock is a freelance writer, blogger, and author of *Memories of Me: A Complete Guide to Telling and Sharing the Stories of Your Life.* In addition to her memory sharing blog at TreasureChestofMemories.com, Ms. Hedgecock is a co-founder and contributing blogger at TheRoadLessWritten.com and frequently guest-posts at other sites. When she's not writing, she enjoys spending time with her husband and two sons, (and her springer spaniel), playing soccer, nature photography, and finding her roots—which might explain her messy house. I include Laura today because of her wonderful blogs and to share a non-fiction view of writing.

***

Justin Sloan: Laura, thank you for sharing your work with us via TheRoadLessWritten.com blog and in this interview. You recently published your first book, titled *Memories of Me: A Complete Guide to Telling and Sharing the Stories of Your Life*. The idea of helping people to capture and write about their memories sounds wonderful, and I enjoyed your touching introduction. My grandfather wrote his memoirs to share with the family, and reading what he had been through changed my life. Everyone should read your book to get the full story, but would you care to share some of that with us here?

Laura Hedgecock: *Memories of Me* guides writers of all experience levels, enabling them to create a legacy of stories and memory episodes. Rather than a how-to-write-a-memoir book, it's a memory-compilers' companion. It introduces topics, sparks recall and creativity with in-depth brainstorming exercises and various writing samples, and provides just enough writing tips for writers to take pride in their projects.

My Grandmother was the inspiration for Memories of Me. She left us a spiral notebook filled with a lifetime of writings, which she called her "Treasure Chest of Memories." *Memories of Me* taps into my grandmother's ideas as well as her passion of connecting with loved ones through memory narratives.

JS: Can you tell me more about the origins of your blog, TreasureChestofMemories.com? Where did the motivation for this come from?

LH: The motivation for blogging content germane to my book came from a need to develop a platform, something that has become an absolute necessity for non-celebrity how-to authors. "Treasure Chest of Memories" was the metaphor that I used to develop my guide, so it seemed a natural fit for my website. Writers decide what kind of "chest" they want to create, what "treasures" they want to put in their chest, as well as how, when, and to what extent they want to share its contents.

JS: Did you know at the time that you were going to write a whole book?

LH: Actually, my completed manuscript led to my website and blog, not vice versa. Rather than a true "author" or "book" site, TreasureChestofMemories.com addresses the same market niche as my book does. It offers tips and resources for those wanting to preserve and share episodes of their pasts.

JS: I see you write quite a lot about writing and the craft of writing. What would be your advice for aspiring writers looking to improve their craft? MFAs? Books on writing (in addition to yours and mine, of course)?

LH: I should note that my book and website are not intended only for professional writers. Thus, most of the advice comes from an "I can do it; you can too!" perspective, rather than from a teacher to student standpoint.

But, maybe that's the best way for authors to support each other. We can share our journeys and explain what helped us most, without implying our way is the best or only way. Other writers can adapt those tactics and strategies that resonate with them.

To your point of resources, my top three favorite resources on writing and style are:

- William Strunk and E.B. White, The Elements of Style, 4th Edition. Longman, 1999. ISBN-13: 9780205313426, ISBN: 0205313426.

- William Zinsser, On Writing Well, 30th Anniversary Edition: Harper, 2012. ISBN-10: 141775057X.

- William Zinsser, Writing About Your Life, Marlow, 2004. ISBN-10: 1569243794.

JS: Now that you have a book out there, what is the biggest struggle?

LH: I have a business background, so I actually like some of the book marketing. The biggest struggle for me is balancing my time and energy between marketing tactics and creating something new.

JS: Having met through the San Francisco Writers Conference, I am curious to know what you enjoyed about the conference and what you would recommend aspiring writers do to prepare.

LH: The San Francisco Writers Conference (SFWC) is justifiably popular because of the access it offers aspiring authors to agents and publishers. However, it offers much more than that. The SFWC also offers access to experts. For instance, Stephanie Chandler helped me brainstorm what my website would look like and Michael Larsen encouraged me to look at smaller publishing houses. And, meeting and networking with other authors can also be tremendously helpful.

I think preparing yourself to go with an open mind might be the best advice I can offer. Absorb everything you can.

I went with what I thought was a polished proposal with the intention of landing an agent. While I was there, I figured out that I didn't have it all figured out, but also went home with great ideas and inspiration.

JS: Having gone with a small press, what would you advise for authors considering small press versus self-publishing? Or would you advise they hold out for an agent and one of the big six?

LH: I would advise writers to separate their own goals from what works best for their book as they take a long, realistic look at their genre, platform, and the publishing landscape. Obviously, you have to make the same choice for each, but pulling yourself out of the equation can give you a lot of clarity. Taking that metaphor a little further, a writer's choice of publishing options is akin to solving a multivariable equation. One you've identified the x and the y, you're closer to your answer. But, unlike math, not everyone will come up with the same solution. It's what works best for you and your book.

In the prescriptive non-fiction (how-to) genre, big houses are only an option for those books whose author already possesses a platform. Because my concept was timely, I didn't think it would serve the book well to wait until I'd built enough of a platform to attract an agent or big house. On the other hand, after researching hundreds of publishers, I found a few that I felt were already serving that niche well, worked with first-time authors, and had a reasonable publishing time-frame. Luckily, my top choice liked my manuscript.

The smaller house was also a good fit for me as an author—and as a person. My book had emotional significance to family members, so hitting that "published" benchmark outweighed potential earnings. Also, having outside expertise appealed to my self-doubting perfectionist side. I didn't want creative control. It was my first book; I was completely overwhelmed with the prospects of choosing editors, cover designers, and proofreaders. Although the business end of marketing a book didn't scare me, I knew I'd need an occasional nudge when it came to promotion.

As it turned out, the smaller house—Cedar Fort Publishing—was the best fit for my goals and the book's future.

JS: Thank you so much for your time, Laura. Before we sign off, do you have any other advice that I may have not asked about? Last minute words of wisdom?

LH: Yes, I have two words of wisdom.

1. Find a tribe or writers support group. Other authors are not your competitors in the traditional sense. If readers like a book similar to yours, chances are they'll like yours too. Look for a group of other writers that can encourage you and help you along the way.

2. Keep in mind that there aren't always "right" or "wrong" choices as you publish and market your books. It's more of a question of finding the right fit for your talent and your works. As you deliberate, think about what really matters to you. Do you want to maximize income or do you want help getting your first work to market? Are you willing and able to put in extra time and effort to maintain creative control? Asking yourself hard questions will help you tremendously as you set your goals and find your way.

Interview: Ron Capps, Founder of the Veterans Writing Project

Ron Capps, a fellow Johns Hopkins MA in writing alum, founded the Veterans Writing Project. I attended a class with the Veterans Writing Project in 2011 and I was blown away. One of my classmates talked about the book (and now film) *We Were Soldiers Once... And Young*, an amazing book and fun film, but the kicker was that this guy was there. He fought among those men. Yet again, a veteran workshop brought tears to my eyes. If you get a chance to attend and are starting off in your writing endeavors, give it a go. If you are not a veteran but want to support this cause, contact Ron and donate. It all helps.

***

Justin Sloan: Thank you for agreeing to share your insight with us today, Ron. What inspired you to start the Veterans Writing Project?

Ron Capps: Wow. Long story. Let me try to be concise. I left the service and went to grad school for writing at JHU. As I was getting close to graduation I knew I wanted to do something with what I was learning, both in graduate school and as a working writer—I was writing for *Foreign Policy* and *TIME* magazine. So I figured I would just give it away. I started the Veterans Writing Project as a way for veterans who were also working writers to give away to other veterans, service members, and their adult family members what we knew as a way of getting those others to write.

JS: And we greatly appreciate you for doing that! It is a wonderful program. How is the program running today?

Do you continue to teach classes, and what is the best way for veterans to get involved?

RC: We absolutely do continue to teach; it is very much our core mission. We run our standard two-day seminars that move participants through the elements of craft—scene, setting, dialogue, narrative structure, plot, point of view, and so on. We run genre specific workshops in fiction, non-fiction and playwriting. And we partner with other organizations to bring training to specialized audiences or in specific venues: we work with Wounded Warrior Project and The Writers Guild Initiative to mentor a group of veterans in San Antonio; we work with The Wilderness Society to take groups of veterans out into wilderness areas and write; we work with the National Endowment for the Arts to teach creative and expressive writing to active service members at Walter Reed National Military Medical Center.

The best way for veterans—and their adult family members— to get involved is to check out our website (veteranswriting.org). We do travel. To date, we've presented in DC, Pennsylvania, several places in North Carolina and several in Virginia, Iowa, Texas, Illinois, Washington State, South Dakota, Arizona, and Massachusetts. We're very interested in bringing our programs to underserved populations of veterans.

JS: That is a wonderful resource. Do you know of any other programs for veterans that want to write?

RC: Well, I mentioned some of the groups we partner with already. Some of us in the VWP have teaching jobs at community colleges and bigger research universities. But we also work with non-academic writing programs like The Writer's Center in Maryland. These are places where someone who doesn't want or need to get a formal, academic writing credential can go and work on specific elements of their work or just get some workshop time in to hone a particular piece of work. There are also groups similar to the VWP around the country: Warrior Writer in Philadelphia, Words after War and several others in NYC, Eileen Schell's veterans writing group in Syracuse... the list goes on and is growing pretty regularly.

Also, there are a number of publishing platforms out there, too. Our journal is *O-Dark-Thirty*. We publish both online and in print. We feature fiction, non-fiction, poetry, plays, and interviews and profiles written by veterans, service members, and adult family members. But there are other platforms out there at Eastern Kentucky University and at the Air Force Academy.

JS: You must have come across some very inspiring stories over the years, is there one or two that you are able to share with us today?

RC: Oh, yeah. I love hearing about and reading the works that come out of our programs or just over the transom for publication in our journal. But rather than focus on one or two individual stories, I'd rather think bigger. The most inspiring story is that we're getting men and women to tell stories that they may not have ever been able to get out. There have been a number of cases where we've had spouses sitting next to each other in a workshop and one of them will read something while the other sits and stares open mouthed and then says, "He (or she) has never even told me that."

I think one of the other big stories is that we're getting groups of veterans together across generations. We've had veterans of World War II, Korea, Vietnam, Cold War, Iraq, and Afghanistan in our seminars and represented in our journal. I think this is really important.

And finally, we're putting this writing out in front of people who might not ever be exposed to it. Less than one percent of Americans took part in the wars in Iraq and Afghanistan, and well under ten percent of Americans are veterans. We're publishing it, but we're also creating an archive of literary writing by veterans—which hasn't been done before.

JS: And of course you have your book *Seriously Not*

Alright: *Five Wars in Ten Years*. It sounds powerful and touching, and I look forward to reading it. Would you like to share some more about the book for our readers?

RC: Sure. I served in the Army and as a Foreign Service Officer for the Department of State for twenty-five years. During the last half of my career I was deployed to five different wars. The book is the story of what that was like, but also the story of what those repeated deployments with insufficient downtime and medical care did to me. It's structured so that we take the reader through the war in Kosovo; then two deployments in Central Africa—in 1996 during the Banyamulenge War in Zaire, and in 1998-2000 in Rwanda dealing with the aftermath of the genocide and the continuing attacks by the Interhamwe into Rwanda—then to Afghanistan in 2002-2003 and Iraq in 2004; the last set of deployments were into Darfur during the genocide there in 2005-2006. The last section of the book is about the aftermath of all that. I was medevac'd out of Darfur and sent home. I really struggled with PTSD but am recovering now, and much of that recovery is due to writing.

JS: Thank you, Ron, for sharing your story and very insightful advice. Before signing off today, do you have any last bits of advice for writers in general, and military veterans specifically?

RC: I guess I say two things. First, if you have a story—and we believe that every veteran does—find a way to tell it. Of course I push writing, but if that's not for you, try music, art, dance, or drama. Use the arts as a way of getting that story out of the back of your mind. And second, don't isolate yourself. We're trained in the military to be a part of a team. But when we come home we're often broken away from that team. So don't isolate yourself. Open up to your family, find a new squad to run with, join a writer's group. Be a part of something that, like the military, is larger than yourself.

Interview: Jerri Bell, Managing Editor of *O-Dark-Thirty*

To further your introduction to the Veterans Writing Project, and for those writers of you interested in editing, I chose to include my interview with Jerri Bell. Jerri was kind enough to share some thoughts with us on the process of editing and how she got to this point. Jerri Bell served in the Navy from 1988-2008. Her fiction has been published in Stone Canoe; her nonfiction has been published in *The Little Patuxent Review* and the *Charleston Gazette-Mail,* and on the *Quivering Pen* and Maryland Humanities Council blogs; and both her fiction and nonfiction have won prizes in the West Virginia Writers annual contests. She is currently the managing editor of *O-Dark-Thirty,* the literary journal of the Veterans Writing Project.

Note: This interview will also appear in my book tentatively titled *Veterans in Creative Careers,* along with many other great military veteran interviews and advice.

***

Justin Sloan: First off, I would like to say that I greatly enjoyed "My First Cinderella Writing Moment" published in *The Quivering Pen* blog, and would love to hear about what you are working on lately. Are you full-time writing and editing? Does the editing ever leave you too exhausted to write your own material?

Jerri Bell: Thanks for reading that essay! I hope you enjoyed *The Quivering Pen,* too. The reviews that David Abrams writes are responsible for more than a third of the books I've bought in the last year. I highly recommend subscribing! Right now I'm writing and editing, but both are part-time occupations. I'm retired with a military pension and my husband, who is supportive of my writing goals, still works full-time; but I'm also the stay-home mom of two teenage boys, and I'm helping my mother, who is disabled, manage several serious health issues. Like most writers, I have to work writing and editing in around other, real-world time commitments.

Editing took my writing in a new direction, a direction that Mark Farrington (of JHU) suggested in the first workshop I took with him, but one that I wasn't ready to pursue at that time. I was still on active duty when I started at JHU in 2005, and I went into graduate school thinking that I could write the Great Navy Novel (cue hysterical laughter).

The protagonist in the chapters that I workshopped with Mark was a young enlisted man. Mark said that I needed to write from the perspective of a female sailor instead. At first I was offended – a writer should be able to write protagonists of either gender. But after some discussion with Mark, I understood that he meant something different. The themes that were coming out in my writing would be more immediate and emotionally resonant with a female protagonist. "I can't write that," I told Mark. "Women in the military don't tell it like it is. If I do, it will just make things worse for other women in the service." I got my commission two years before Tailhook, and we all watched Lieutenant Paula Coughlin get crucified in public and in private for speaking up. So I honestly believed that silence would prevent setbacks in gender integration in the military.

Fast-forward into the summer of 2013. Veterans Writing Program founder Ron Capps (also a JHU grad) and I were discussing the reasons that women veterans in our seminars don't speak up or share their work like the men do. We see it all the time. Ron asked me why I thought it was happening, and challenged me to think about what I might do to make a difference in a seminar specifically for women veterans. I knew exactly why women weren't speaking up, and I started noodling around with a seminar unit on risk-taking, women, and writing. About the same time, the press renewed coverage of military sexual trauma (MST); and I realized that women's silence about discrimination and harassment translates to a kind of voluntary complicity. Keeping our mouths shut was professionally necessary when I was serving, but in the end we didn't stop the behavior with our silence. We drove it further underground.

I also realized that I couldn't teach women veterans about taking risks with their writing if I wasn't willing to take risks with my own. In response to a contest sponsored by Words After War, I wrote an essay on having survived a violent sexual assault before I joined the Navy, and on what it was like to deal with the aftereffects when I was working with pilots in the pre-Tailhook era. The essay won the competition, and was later picked up for publication in the Summer 2014 issue of *Little Patuxent Review*. Now I'm going back to short fiction to revisit some of the themes I was afraid to explore through the eyes of a female protagonist. The first story should be ready for submission in a couple of weeks.

Editing energizes my writing in other ways. I didn't graduate from Hopkins into an established community of writers: my classmates were all adult professionals, spread out all over Metro DC and the Baltimore area, and after grad school we melted back into our professional communities and established lives. Editing has brought me back into a writing community whose members share a common background and similar interests, and it keeps me focused on the importance of storytelling and the need to speak and to be heard. It also reminds me to slow down and make everything I submit as good as I possibly can, and to follow good submission etiquette (professional cover letters, matching the work to the publication, and proofreading to the best of my ability before I hit "send").

Sometimes when we're copyediting our quarterly print journal, I wish I could spend less time checking punctuation and usage and more time working on my stories! But reading and writing are the warp and weft in the fabric of the writing life. None of the effort is wasted.

JS: I am glad the path has led you here—it sounds like a challenging one! Many of us fiction writers would love to become involved in literary journals in an editorial capacity. How did you find yourself involved with *O-Dark-Thirty*? Have you edited for other journals or fiction of any sort in the past?

JB: I'd heard before I graduated in 2009 that a fellow student veteran was planning to found a program for veteran writers, and I squirreled that information away somewhere in the back of my mind. One night almost four years later I found a short profile of the Veterans Writing Project, Ron Capps, and *O-Dark-Thirty* in *Poets & Writers*. I jumped out of bed, read the entire VWP web site, and then e-mailed Ron my writing bio and asked how I could get involved. He made me the managing editor for our online journal.

The only thing I'd edited before that was the local elementary school newsletter. I hope the teachers were sending nonfiction inputs! That editing job felt useful, but it didn't invoke the same joy that I feel every time I hit the "accept" button in Submittable and tell another fellow veteran that we're going to make him or her a published author. I've been lucky to work with three other editors, all military veterans and JHU graduates (Jim Mathews, fiction; Dario DiBattista, nonfiction; and Fred Foote, poetry) who have been generous with their time and patient with the million questions I've had to ask about *O-Dark-Thirty's* standards and working with authors to learn the editing job.

JS: How would you advise other writers seek out such opportunities? Is there anything they should do to prepare themselves, such as study editing techniques, or is studying the craft of writing enough?

JB: If there are "editing techniques" to study, I hope someone will send me a list! I can use all the help I can get.

Studying the craft of writing is essential. Craft is the toolbox for both writers and editors. Before I got involved with *O-Dark-Thirty*, I'd been blogging about short stories as a way of studying craft and teaching myself to articulate what worked and didn't work for me as a reader. Being able to articulate areas for improvement, especially in a constructive way, is an important skill for an editor to have. And an editor has to be a giver. An editor has to want to publish other people's work, and be willing to help other writers do their best. It's important to see oneself as part of a community of collaborators, not as another predator in the Sea of Publishing whose job is to keep the gate against one's writing competitors. Sending rejections is unavoidable, but I find it helpful to focus on saying "yes" to as many writers as possible and encouraging the rest to keep working and submitting. I don't want to be the kind of editor who grooves on voting other writers off the literary island, so to speak.

I'd advise other writers to read as many publications as they can in their area of interest—especially regional and small journals—and to network at writing conferences whenever possible. And keep writing and submitting! Getting something published or winning a contest tells a senior editor that you at least have some clue about the basics of submission and publication. Then, when you find a journal that publishes work you love, write to the senior editor and ask if they'd consider taking you on as a reader. Be willing to work for little or no money at first.

JS: Let's move on to how this all affects the writer. What would you say an editor looks for in the initial stages of submission, when searching for focus or content?

JB: Every editor out there would have a slightly different answer to that question.

As managing editor, my first job is to screen for conformity with our submission guidelines. O-Dark-Thirty publishes fiction, nonfiction and poetry only from a certain segment of the writing population. If the submitter hasn't made their affiliation with the armed forces clear in the cover letter, I have to send an e-mail requesting clarification. At *O-Dark-Thirty* we aren't going to reject out-of-hand a submission that's a couple of hundred words over our limit, is not in Times New Roman 12, or is not perfectly punctuated. But the editors of many publications are going to make their first cut based on exactly those kinds of things.

I tend to be a "second reader" at *O-Dark-Thirty*. If the title, the writer's bio, or the first couple of lines catch my attention—or if we've already seen work from that writer before—I will probably give the submission a quick initial read. But I forward it on to the appropriate "adjudicating" editor without comment unless something in the cover letter needs clarification, the submitter has a history with us, or something in that quick scan has me excited as a reader. If a second opinion is needed, I'm happy to re-read and collaborate with the fiction and nonfiction editors. (I would be the last person to offer an opinion on a poem, though I'm getting better at understanding what Fred sees in the poems that he chooses for publication.)

When I'm reading to provide that second opinion, the first thing I'm looking for is an authentic voice. There's a joke that all sea stories start with the phrase, "This is a no-shitter." I want to hear that confidence, that tone that the writer first and foremost has a story worth telling, that the authorial voice has...authority. In our August issue, both Sylvia Bowersox ("This War Can't Be All Bad") and Greg White ("The Lead Weight") nailed that tone, in my reading ear.

I'm open to almost any content. *O-Dark-Thirty* isn't just a publication for military-themed work, though the majority of submissions we receive are in some way related to military service.

JS: How would you say this work in the initial stage differs from the final steps for publication? Does it differ? How much do you look at changing actual content in either stage, and how do you relate to a writer at the different stages?

JB: I'm never interested in changing content. If I ask a submitter to make changes, the changes have to be theirs and not mine. Otherwise, in my opinion, we're asking the writer to violate the integrity of the work. I may ask him or her to focus more on some aspect of craft, to consider alternative structures, or to develop something in the writing more fully. But it's not my job to tell the writer what to write. I hope that in reading both fiction and nonfiction, I'm able to see things in a manuscript that the writer might not have realized were there. Things that could make the story "more" of what it aims to be.

Occasionally, I ask for large changes. "The Lead Weight" was rewritten with excerpts from several chapters of Greg White's memoir manuscript to make it publishable as a stand-alone piece. I couldn't use any individual chapter by itself. Greg and I talked at great length about structure, conflict, image, and especially theme. I didn't want to change his wonderful voice, or his story: he's a comedy writer for television, and he's really funny. But the material he was dealing with carried weight well beyond his clever punch lines, and we worked together to bring that deeper meaning forward and to give it greater resonance as we developed the excerpt. I'm not sure that he fully realized the significance or potential impact of what he was writing until we started trying to decide what part of the memoir to publish.

I always reserve the right to change an author's use of commas unless the usage is a key aspect of voice. I hate comma usage errors.

JS: Would this process differ for an editor of novels, in your opinion?

JB: Having neither edited nor published a novel or a book-length nonfiction manuscript, I'm not sure. I would think that it's similar, but in a long work there would be so many more potential areas for enhancement. E. L. Doctorow describes writing a novel as driving across the country at night: you can only see as far as your headlights. An editor sitting down with a long manuscript would probably be reading for, among other things, the totality of the journey. So I suspect that the editor of a longer work would be very concerned with how cohesive the entire manuscript was, and would have to spend more time on pacing and continuity than an editor of short pieces.

JS: I can't begin to understand how I would edit someone else's novel. As a fiction writer, what do you think about editors? I ask because I still find them quite terrifying— they are the gatekeepers, in a way, or one of many gatekeepers. Do you worry about editors changing your material, or is it really more about smoothing it out?

JB: The editors of literary journals that have requested changes to my work have offered suggestions that made the manuscript better. I haven't yet had one ask me to make a change that I couldn't stomach. I'll give you two examples below. The submissions were nonfiction, but I think I would feel the same way about fiction submissions if I had a good vibe from the editor.

Emily Rich at *Little Patuxent Review* saw immediately that when I wrote about the effect of surviving a violent sexual assault, I had barely mentioned the initial incident. She challenged me, in a kind and respectful way, to share as much as I felt comfortable sharing about it with readers. Her rationale was that knowing about the initial assault would make readers more invested in my story, give them a better understanding of the stakes, and give them more reason to care about my character and the aftermath of the assault. She was exactly right. The paragraph that I added may have been the most difficult paragraph I've ever written: it wasn't easy to get naked literally and figuratively on the page, and to let readers right into my bed on a really bad night. But the impact on the story I was trying to tell was positive and immense. It was still my story after the change she suggested. It was even more my story, if that makes sense.

And the same is true for Amber Jensen, the editor I'm currently working with at *The Journal of Military Experience*. She knows how to make writing better without altering what's important to a writer. We're working together on an essay that I wasn't happy with, but didn't want to give up on. She saw immediately what was missing, but has given me the space to try to make the necessary changes in my own way. She isn't dictating what I should write; she has just pointed out what I could do better and expressed confidence that I could do it. I've come to recognize that I can't always see either the weaknesses or the strengths in what I've written, and I am deeply grateful to the editors whose vision exceeds and enhances mine.

JS: I am convinced, and will certainly look to editors for bringing my work to the next level. Well, Jerri, this has been extremely helpful and I want to think you again for your time. On a last parting word, what do you see yourself doing in the near future? Any exciting projects of yours we should know about?

JB: I'm excited that the discussions Ron Capps and I had about a writing workshop just for women veterans have finally come to fruition. The Veterans Administration Medical Center in Washington, DC has a new Women's Center that's sponsoring the workshop, which is running from September to December. I very much enjoy helping other women veterans take risks and tell their stories—to whatever audience they please, in whatever way they please. I hope we'll be able to continue offering the workshop, perhaps in additional locations. Our stories matter too, and it's time for us to break the silence.

CONCLUSION

Alas, I must leave you now. I leave you with my advice on how to position yourself for a writing career. Even better, I leave you with the advice from all of the super intelligent people who agreed to include their interviews in this book. Your next task is, at risk of sounding repetitive, to get out there and write. Put together your career plan, relook at it after considering what you have read here, and make some changes to the plan. When you are done with it, hang it on your wall where you can see it and make sure to glance over at it every once in a while. It will be so fulfilling when you walk past that plan in a few years (or sooner, or later—who knows) and see that it is time to cross some items off the list of dreams and mark them as realities. Revise your resume and LinkedIn. Build up your network, attend some classes, be open to new ideas and projects, and most of all write like crazy and revise even crazier to improve your craft. Good luck in the job search!

Best,

Justin M. Sloan

www.JustinMSloan.com

SloanArtist@gmail.com

ANNEX A: RESOURCES

Books: On Film and Television

- *Screenplay: The Foundations of Screenwriting*, Syd Field
- *How to Break in to TV Writing: Insider Interviews*, Gray Jones
- *Getting it Write: An Insider's Guide to a Screenwriting Career*, Lee Jessup
- *Riding the Alligator*, Pen Densham
- *Pixar's 22 Rules of Story, Analyzed*, Stephan Bugaj
- *Writing Screenplays that Sell*, Michael Hauge
- *Four Screenplays*, William Goldman
- *Adventures in the Screen Trade*, William Goldman
- *The Screenwriters Bible: A Complete Guide to Writing, Formatting, and Selling Your Script*, David Trottier
- *Story: Style, Structure, Substance, and the Principles of Screenwriting*, Robert McKee
- *Save the Cat*, Blake Snyder
- *Writing Movies for Fun and Profit: How We Made a Billion Dollars at the Box Office and You Can, Too!*, Thomas Lennon and Robert Ben Garant
- *Your Screenplay Sucks: 100 Ways to Make it Great*, William M. Akers
- *Lew Hunter's Screenwriting 434: The Industry's Premier Teacher Reveals the Secrets of the Successful*

Screenplay, Lew Hunter

- *Screenwriting: The Sequence Approach*, Paul Guilino
- *The Writer's Journey: Mythic Structure for Storytellers & Screenwriters*, Christopher Vogler

Books: On Video Games

- *Video Game Storytelling: What Every Developer Needs to Know*, Evan Skolnick
- *The Ultimate Guide to Video Game Writing and Design*, Flint Dille and John Zuur Platten
- *Video Game Writing*, Maurice Suckling
- *Writing for Video Games*, Steve Ince
- *Professional Techniques for Video Game Writing*, Wendy Despain

Books: On Fiction

- *The Breakout Novelist: Craft and Strategies for Career Fiction Writers*, Donald Maass
- *Writing Tools: 50 Essential Strategies for Every Writer*, Roy Peter Clark
- *Reading Like a Writer: A Guide for People Who Love Books and for Those Who Want to Write Them*, Francine Prose
- *How Fiction Works*, James Woods
- *Self Editing for Fiction Writers*, Renni Browne and Dave King
- *The Art of Fiction*, John Gardner
- *On Becoming a Novelist*, John Gardner

- *The Art of Fiction*, Ann Rand
- *Immediate Fiction*, Jerry Cleaver
- *On Writing*, Stephen King
- *The First Five Pages*, Noah Lukeman
- *Writing War: A Guide to Telling Your Own Story*, Ron Capps
- *The Hero with a Thousand Faces*, Joseph Campbell

Books: Non-fiction

- *Memories of Me: A Complete Guide to Telling and Sharing the Stories of Your Life*, Laura Hedgecock
- *Creative Nonfiction: Researching and Crafting Stories of Real Life*, Philip Gerard
- *Writing Creative Nonfiction*, Philip Gerard
- *You Can't Make This Stuff Up: The Complete Guide to Writing Creative Nonfiction, from Memoir to Literary Journalism*, Lee Gutkind
- *Telling True Stories: A Nonfiction Writers' Guide from the Nieman Foundation at Harvard University*, Mark Kramer and Wendy Call
- *Storycraft: The Complete Guide to Writing Narrative Nonfiction*, Jack Hart

Video Games to Play

- *The Walking Dead* (Telltale Games)
- *The Wolf Among Us* (Telltale Games)
- *Game of Thrones* (Telltale Games)
- *Tales from the Borderlands* (Telltale Games)

- *Heavy Rain* (Quantic Dream)
- *Beyond Two Souls* (Quantic Dream)
- *Last of Us* (Naughty Dog)
- *Uncharted* (Naughty Dog)
- *South Park: The Stick of Truth* (Obsidian Entertainment/ Ubisoft)
- *To the Moon* (Freebird Games)
- *Year Walk* (iOS game and companion app)
- *Dead Space* (EA)
- *Grand Theft Auto V* (Rockstar Games)
- *Red Dead Redemption* (Rockstar Games)
- *Mass Effect* (BioWare)
- *Bioshock* (Irrational Games)

ANNEX B: INTERVIEW WITH JUSTIN SLOAN,

EVILTENDER.COM

I have included this interview for those of you that want more information on the Austin Film Festival, in the form of an interview in which I was the interviewee, for a change. It is dated, but still largely applicable. The interview was conducted by Chris Jalufka and can be found on the EvilTender.com website.

As a note of timeliness, this interview was conducted some time ago. The short film has been completed, and the feature has met a version of development hell. I hope you find the interview useful regardless, and so have included it below.

Interview at: http://eviltender.com/2013/02/21/a-writers-perspective-justin-sloan

***

Interview: A Writer's Perspective, Justin Sloan

To fully experience everything that happens at the Austin Film Festival you need stamina and a willingness to just go for it– meaning, a movie is starting at 6:00 p.m. that you know nothing about and there's a party right after it but you just got out of panel and you stop to think, 'Did I eat lunch yet?' and of course you haven't. You buddy up with a few perfect strangers and head to the theater because you know that popcorn is a decent lunch anyway.

My own stamina and willingness would falter, but there was always something there to inspire me to keep going. Wake up early, stay out late. Nonstop. One of the inspirations was fellow writer and second rounder at the festival, Justin Sloan. We met at the first opening afternoon party and he'd be the impetus for many a late night.

Justin is a former Marine and former actor who works for the Federal Reserve doing something major with finance and Asia, a career that is far over my head, but just understood enough to make me feel like an inadequate underachiever. He also happens to write screenplays and novels in his spare time that have placed in various contests and festivals.

Part of what made the Austin Film Festival such a great experience was meeting other writers like Justin Sloan, where we can congregate and share our experiences, struggles, and goals. Rushing through the streets of Austin talking writing definitely adds a spark to the already burning fire inside, the one that keeps you writing and creating when the world only offers reasons to extinguish and move on.

I caught up with Justin to talk projects, contests, and fitting writing between the gaps of family and career.

ET: You were in the Marine Corps for five years before attending the School of Advanced International Studies (SAIS) at Johns Hopkins University. Did you join the Marines right out of high school? Was that a hard decision? Was there a plan in play there?

JS: When I graduated high school I thought I could either try to go to college on student loans to study art, or go with my best friend to join the Marines and figure out college later. I was under the impression that it is unrealistic to pursue one's artistic passions, which led me to the choice to join the Marines.

I left the day after graduating high school and it was in many ways a great experience. However, now I've reached a point in my life where I realize that we should follow our passions. To try to ignore them to fit into society and have a normal job may lead to a satisfied life, but it leaves something wanting. I certainly do not regret joining the Marines as that experience brought me into acting and is a large part of my motivation when writing. But it was a tough five years!

The SAIS program at Johns Hopkins is an incredibly difficult program to be accepted into. What attracted you to apply?

I studied abroad in Japan in my senior year at the University of California, San Diego. Once again I was faced with how to obtain a normal nine to five job that could support a family, so I decided to apply to graduate schools. Another factor in play was the fact that I was enlisted in the military, not an officer. This meant people who knew nothing but had degrees were telling me what to do!

Naturally I had an inferiority complex, so I decided to go after all the education I could. I even considered PhD programs for a while, but realized that energy could go into writing fiction instead, and therefore decided to stop after my SAIS degree.

At the time I applied, I had high aspirations of working at the Treasury Department or Federal Reserve as an Asia analyst (I am doing the latter now). It worked and I feel incredibly blessed. And of course there was the fact that SAIS allows the first year of graduate school to be in Bologna, Italy. How could I pass up that opportunity?

Like the Marines, this experience has influenced my writing and one of my screenplays takes place partially in Bologna. Everything somehow works its way into the writing.

A career at the Federal Reserve is a pretty major deal. I mean, some people work incredibly hard just to reach that point. Since having met you at the Austin Film Festival I've seen that you put just as much effort into your writing. Is the plan to have two careers, or is writing the ultimate goal?

I thought long and hard about this question, and at the

moment I lean towards a two track life style. Instead of one or the other, putting all my energy into writing or my career at the Federal Reserve, why not just work twice as hard and do both? So that is indeed the plan.

The hard part is that now I have a newborn daughter, so I have to stretch myself in three directions – it hurts! If someday I am incredibly successful as a writer of fiction and screenplays, I would have to enter into a new stage of life-pondering and make a decision at that point. But for now, having a job that has nothing to do with writing fiction certainly gives me experiences that can influence my fiction and time spent wishing I could write, so that when I do write I am incredibly enthusiastic about it.

I saw the other day a quote about sitting down to write being difficult and I have to say I completely disagree – it is those moments spent not writing that are difficult because we want to write so bad.

Yeah, by time I get home from work and finish up whatever chores there are to do around the house, sitting down to write is a great feeling. How do balance your career and family while still finding time to write?

Writing with a child is tough! Craig Mazin and John August discuss this on their Scriptnotes podcast, and I have to agree. There are no more writing until three in the morning marathons. If I am lucky I get some time in the evenings and weekends, but I make sure to wake up early every day and get in about thirty minutes of revision in the morning before leaving for work, and then another thirty minutes of writing on the Bart on my way to work. It is tough, but I am still making progress. And of course, having a daughter is amazing and inspiring.

I remember Ashley Edward Miller (*Thor, X-Men: First Class*) saying that if his kid wakes up at 6:30AM, he gets up at 4:30AM to write. I'm not much of an early riser, but

when a kid comes my way I'm planning on changing that.

You spent some time as an actor. How does that fit into the timeline between the Marine Corps, Johns Hopkins, and now? Is that something that you're still pursuing, or have you moved on?

My time as an actor actually came about because of the Marine Corps. Marines that went to boot camp in San Diego are called 'Hollywood Marines' by some, and I certainly lived up to that. One of my supervisors, a Major, was an activated reservist after the early post-9-11 days. His full time job when not working with the Marines was as an actor. He had small parts in movies like 'Bruce Almighty,' and had a nice career in small budget horror movies.

He told me something I had not realized about Hollywood, which was that you don't have to be super attractive or tall or all that jazz to be an actor. So my coworker and I started going to auditions and taking acting classes. We had a blast! I was in at least ten student and independent films, including my one IMDB credit on a film titled *Alien Abduction*. I only had three lines in that one, and at the time it came out I had finished my five years in the Marines and had to decide whether to continue trying to act or study abroad in Japan.

I had always loved Japan, and decided I could always come back to acting. So I went off to spend a year in Tokyo, where I did a few small acting gigs. Unfortunately, the acting slowly faded from my life as I focused my energy towards finding a career. I can't say I won't go back to it someday. I loved acting almost as much as I love to write.

When you begin a script how concerned are you with its commercial appeal? What audience do you consider the priority—the script readers of competitions, potential filmmakers, or the end user who will hopefully see the film on the screen?

What a tough question! When I approach a script or a novel

or any writing endeavor, it is much less about the commercial appeal for me than it is about a burning need to write the story. By the time I sit down to write, the story has been marinating in my brain (and in various notebooks and computer files) for quite some time. So I write the story I want to write, and then on the rewrite I tend to think about the scenes in terms of what would a script reader say.

In that sense I suppose my writing has meandered towards catering to the readers, but I recently started writing a script on Japan that deals with a guy running away from America because he does not know how to deal with the fact that a girl he loves has cancer. I am writing it how I want, script readers be darned! And if it doesn't sell, I write it as a novel and sell that. So it varies for me in that I will write some scripts with more of a commercial angle in mind, and some for the artistic, passionate side of myself.

Beyond entering script competitions, you've really put your work out there and two of your scripts are in the process of being made. How did you go about getting your scripts in the hands of filmmakers?

To once again refer to Scriptnotes, Craig Mazin always says to not write for free. But guess what Mr. Mazin, some of us cannot get a start in the business or see our movies get made if we don't start from such a lowly place as working for free. That is what I have done.

I actually answered an ad in Craigslist to work on a webisode, and when the producer liked my work he asked if I would be interested in collaborating on a feature with him. I first clarified the likelihood of the film getting made. He assured me (as did his credits on IMDB), that it would get made as long as I did a good job and we wrote history!

Okay, we wrote a micro-budget horror, but it was a fun experience and I look forward to seeing how it turns out.

On other scripts I have been receiving read requests through posting my information on MovieBytes.com, winning screenplay contests such as ScriptVamp and The-Greenlight and placing well in Page, Austin, and Creative World Awards, and querying. I am also trying the new Blacklist service, and have my fingers crossed.

In a way my fiction writing is another way I am working to get my scripts out there. My novel version of *Bringer of Light*, which I also have in screenplay format (logline on www.JustinMSloan.com), is in the final round of the San Francisco Writers Conference writing contest, and still in the running. If a story works, I prefer to write it as a screenplay and a novel, because (a) who knows which will sell first, and (b) they are so different it is like exploring your characters all over again but from different angles.

What was the conference like?

The San Francisco Writers Conference was amazing! It was four days of meeting wonderful agents, editors, and fellow authors. I was very surprised at how approachable and friendly all the agents and everyone were, and I will definitely be back next year. I left feeling very inspired, and with several requests for my middle grade novel *Bringer of Light*. I have adapted this novel into a screenplay as well, and it was a finalist in last year's Reel Authors screenplay contest.

We were both in Austin for the Austin Film Festival, and my mind changes constantly about my time there. It was a total blast, but overall I can't say helped, other than to reiterate the fact that we all already know—making a career as a screenwriter is near impossible. What did you think of the festival? Is it something that you would do again?

While I can't say attending the Austin Film Festival one time brought my writing career to a new level, I didn't expect it to. But I made some contacts and I loved the experience. I will certainly return, because I believe it is a great place to be inspired and I hope that making those contacts and continuing to attend each year will help my career.

Since I hope to have a published novel and a produced movie when I go this year, I wonder if the experience will be different. Making it as a screenwriter may be tough, especially if that is all one does, but it is 100 percent impossible if we don't try at all. So I am going to keep writing and make sure to attend the Austin Film Festival every year. I can't wait for the next one!

One of your projects in pre-production is the feature *Live Bait*. How'd you find that project?

Live Bait came about from a Craigslist ad. I recommend that your readers be selective though – it seems like 50 percent of those are scams and another 49 percent may or may not actually get your film made. I could be wrong, I hope the odds are better.

I've never check Craigslist for filmmakers, but you're a lot braver than I am. What's the process like? Are you working from an idea of yours or the filmmakers?

On this script the director/producer came to me with a two paragraph outline of what he was going for and some of the first act written. I asked if I could go my own way with it and revise as I saw fit, and he gave me the go ahead. This is important when working with someone else's idea, you have to be able to make it your own in some way. So I set out to do a sort of *American Pie* meets *From Dusk Till Dawn* (there are no vampires, but something evil and in some ways similar). Given the extremely small budget the film may not live up to those films, but I have faith in my director that it will be great for what it is.

You're also rewriting a short script of yours for another group of filmmakers. How close are you to getting that one up and running?

My short script is very exciting for me because it has been dancing around in the confines of my brain for so long. It finally hit the paper and I love it! Luckily it seems some of the members of this group of filmmakers do too. We met in early February and they seem likely to make the film and even let me direct (I may co-direct as I have never directed before). Keep an eye on my website for updates!

How involved are you in the production of both of these films? Do you plan on being on set?

The great thing about working with both these groups is the people. They are very collaborative and open to ideas. James Tucker is doing my feature film and told me I can come down to LA and be on set, and as I mentioned I may actually direct the short. My roadblocks come from the fact that I have a family and a two month old daughter and that I live in Northern California. That is something we shall have to remedy, isn't it?

It's awesome that you have so many projects in the works. Do you have any interest in producing some of your work yourself? Doing all the funding, producing, casting, etc.?

As a writer, my interest lies primarily in writing. That said, I am working with some filmmakers to produce a short I wrote and may direct. A short seems to be a good reference tool, like a business card you can post online and point others to. I also hope it gets into film festivals like Austin and therefore serve as another talking point. Who knows, maybe someone will see it and approach me about writing a feature? But when it comes to feature films, my plan is to stick to writing them and see what happens.

Beyond scripts you also write fiction and have had your short stories published. How do you choose if a story idea is better off as a short story versus a script?

When considering the canvas for a story I generally approach it with this question in mind: Is this an internal or external story? Meaning, to tell this story do I have to really get into the head of the character, or is this something I can tell through action and dialogue?

I wrote a short story I am trying to get published, based on my cousin who committed suicide. I try to get into the character's mindset and show how estranged she is, how cut off from the sense of family she enjoyed as a child. Could this be done in a feature film? Sure, probably, but it is not the sort of film I enjoy writing and the goal is served much better in a ten to fifteen page short story, in my opinion.

I mentioned earlier the script I am writing on Japan, and you may be thinking that story would be better as a novel or short story. But for me that story is a visual piece, better told through the images of the man's life and his struggles. Considering it now, I see it is a fine line. I have also recently delved into poetry, and that is a different ball game altogether. Poetry is tough!

One thing I've noticed about how you work is the constant movement of your projects. You always have something going on — from writing groups to meetings with filmmakers. At the Austin Film Festival you were at every party and used each moment there to be involved in anything you could. You can see that level of work as well from your time as a Marine, in SAIS, and your acting and career in finance. What keeps this drive of yours going? What keeps you inspired?

I've never been incredibly smart, some may even call me slow (I know who you all are). But one thing I've never been accused of is lacking passion and ambition. I need to believe that if we struggle and never give up we can succeed, because otherwise so many of us are doomed. When I look at other people's success stories, I see this is true!

And when I look back at my life so far, I believe I have demonstrated that to an extent – but not enough. So in part I suppose I work hard to prove to the world that yet another kid from a divorced family of mediocre income can make it.

And then of course there is simply the desire to create. I used to kickbox and I loved it, but at the end of the day what do I have to show for it? A video on Youtube of me kicking some guy's butt and hips that will hurt me until the day I die. But with writing and academic pursuits we can leave something behind for others to enjoy. We can make a difference.

ANNEX C: HOW TO APPROACH THE AUSTIN FILM FESTIVAL

Many of my friends and acquaintances have asked me questions about how the film festival works, what to do to prepare, and how to see what movies are available. Therefore, I want to delve deeper into the Austin Film Festival specifically.

In general you should prepare to have fun and drink lots of coffee. I was exhausted! Of course, I stayed a mile away at the Super 8 (I think it was only $70 a night there). Regardless, you will be running around to different presentations, and in some of the smaller rooms (like the one where one of the Pixar presentations was held when I attended), you will be standing.

In the Driskill Bar and other networking locations, such as the special parties if you have the Conference or Producers badge, the celebrity writers seem totally cool with you approaching them. I think they look at this as the reason they are there. If they didn't want to be approached, they would find their own spot with the other writers and ditch us wannabes. When you approach them, be friendly. Maybe just a "Hi, my name is X, and I appreciate your work. I just wanted to say hello. I am incredibly excited about your upcoming film Y. What are your thoughts on BLAH BLAH?" That could work, but what you should NOT do is try to pitch them your story ideas. Chat, be friendly, and politely dismiss yourself after 30 seconds or so, unless they seem to be having a blast and you think you might have just met your BFF. If you do meet your new BFF networking with a celebrity like this, introduce me and let's go grab some drinks in that special secret bar somewhere!

For films, I recommend you go to the ones with filmmakers in attendance (as stated on the schedule). Otherwise, you might as well see the film at the theater back home or on Netflix, right? But here in Austin you get actors and directors to talk to you about the process, and maybe do the Q&A. That is awesome! But you must arrive at the theater 30 minutes or so in advance, because there are often lines. For the Vince Gilligan script reading with Will Ferrell, I was just at the cutoff point—and it was a two-hour line, if not longer. You will have to juggle your time between attending the presentations you really want to attend and getting to the theater in time. I had free time when I missed presentations I wanted to see, but my fellow attendees and I ended up making this free time our dinner or beer time, so it was not a total loss.

Presentations are the meat of the Austin Film Festival. Go to them, take notes, learn your craft, and introduce yourself to the person beside you. I would say you should not miss the following speakers if you see their names come up in any event descriptions: Craig Mazin, John August, Ashley Miller, and Terry Rossio (there are many more events you should attend, but I am highlighting some of my top picks). The schedule varies from year to year, but a good place to check is in the DoneDealPro forums. Someone will always be discussing the Austin Film Festival there.

The special parties are wonderful for networking, especially since the price of the beer is generally included with the badge. John August was the host of the first party I attended my first year, which meant he was hanging out talking to everyone. (He must have been so tired by the end of the night.) John was super friendly, and I am glad I got the special badge that allowed me to attend his party. That said, the Driskill bar is perfect for networking and does not require one of the more expensive badges to get in. You may find you want to stay the whole weekend on a couch in the bar, and I would not blame you. Some of the parties get way too crowded for my blood, so you will probably see me at the couch next to you if that is where you end up.

The roundtables are worth attending, because you sit at a table with just you and a few other wannabes and talk with professional writers almost one-on-one (taking turns). You sit at one table and the professionals rotate, so you are able to meet with three or so different professionals in the one hour you are in the room. One year I was able to talk with some folks from Pixar, and they were super helpful. Next I spoke with some television writers, which was educational even though I had never heard of them nor had I watched their shows. So there is that element of potentially not knowing who the experts are, but it cannot be avoided because you are not able to pick which professionals come to your table. You are allowed to sign up for just one of these sessions, but if you go to the others you may be able to get in to more. Furthermore, second-rounders and above in the screenplay contest are able to attend two roundtables (their special one and one regular roundtable event).

If you enter the screenplay contest and make it through to the second round or beyond, there are events just for you. From what I have seen, these events do not seem to differ too much from the regular events. A problem with them some years is that they are mostly or all on Friday, which is unfortunate for those of us just going for the weekend. If you can attend the "First Ten Pages" event with Lindsay Duran, do so. You will likely learn that, while you may have made the top 10% or higher, you and the others there still have a long way to go.

The Austin Film Festival pitch event made me a bit nervous at first, but after I was done it was quite fun. You sit in a small room with about thirty people and listen to them pitch. Then you get your turn, so you stand in front of them and a table with a couple of judges (one of mine didn't show up), and get one minute to pitch. They are strict with that minute, but if you talk California-fast like I do, you do not have to worry about the timing, you just have to worry about sounding nervous. If you pass this round, you can compete in the pitch finale at a bar in front of many more people. Either way you should attend this party, and get there early. One year we even got to see John August and Ashley Miller, among others, perform a little pitch game.

The awards lunch will certainly inspire you, but beware—they seem to seat newbies in the back where you can't see. My first year, I had pillars and waiters in my way for half the lunch, and even when my view was not obstructed I could not make out the faces of the presenters. Everyone at my table was a first-timer. I had to look at the program to see the name of the famous actor who was talking to me (it was Robert Patrick, the T-1000 in *Terminator 2*, by the way). The food was great, and they had a nice presentation in honor of Frank Darabont (*The Shawshank Redemption*). I would consider going again for sure if I had the Conference or Producers badge so I could be sure to meet and mingle with even more great people.

Speaking of the great people you will meet there, my first year at the festival Richard Michael Lucas (a second-rounder in 2012) kind of served as my Austin Film Festival mentor. He has attended the CS Expo eight times (considered by some to be the Austin Film Festival's competitor due to competing time slots), and this year will be his third time attending the Austin Film Festival. He had the following advice to pass on:

"I think for the first year/time, it's good to get out of the hotel environment at night, go to the parties, explore a little of the city, and meet a ton of people. It's good for balance. During the day, you will have plenty of time for seminars, panels, impromptu lunch meetings, and networking. After year one, this type of exposure makes it much easier to reevaluate your strategy, strengthen friendships made, plan, and focus on a narrower set of goals. Be polite, professional, and open to making connections on multiple levels; even professional writers. Honor the professionals' time and efforts. They're exposing themselves and sharing great info. Respecting them as people is important in keeping the overall vibe of Austin Film Festival positive. Focus on craft and relationships. Ninety-nine percent of the time, deals are not made at a festival by anyone. But long-lasting impressions are!"

In conclusion: go and have fun, but do not attend thinking that you are going to sell yourself or necessarily advance your career. That said, you might do both. It happens. And if you want to know what to bring, I recommend the following:

- Business Cards: Best for handing to other writers at your level, to keep in touch. Not so much for the experts—Craig Mazin may think you are a tool if you try to give him one.

- Comfortable shoes: For walking all over and standing long hours.

- Tylenol: In case you drink too much at the Driskill bar.

- Cool clothes: It was pretty warm last year (high 70s to low 80s, if I recall correctly).

- A prepared pitch, in case anyone asks. Make it conversational, so you don't sound like a robot. And don't try to pitch everyone. Instead, be ready to talk about your script if someone asks; because I'm pretty sure someone will (even if it is just me).

ANNEX D: GUEST INTERVIEW WITH A SCRIPT READER

The following is an interview conducted by Paul Zeidman (interviewed in Part Four of this book), for his blog Maximum Z. Paul's blog is a wonderful resource for tips on screenwriting and to follow his lessons from his own writing. He also has a series of interviews such as the one that follows, so if you enjoy this interview, head over to his site and read some more.

Interview at: https://maximumz.wordpress.com/?s=norris

***

Ask a Wicked-Smart Script Consultant!

October 14, 2014

The latest in a series of interviews with script readers and consultants who would be worth your while to work with if you want to get your script in shape. Today's spotlight is on Rebecca Norris of Script Reader Pro.

1. What's the last thing you read/watched that you thought was incredibly well- written?

My current obsession is *House of Cards*. At first, I didn't care for the show. I found the device of Francis talking directly to camera a bit odd, the plot lines confusing, and I didn't like any of the characters! However, a friend encouraged me to keep watching, and I'm so glad I pushed through. The genius of the show is in the slow reveals—they don't hand you anything up front—you earn carefully-placed insights into the characters over time. I ended up binge-watching all of Season Two and am now deprived of new episodes until January! I should have spaced them out more.

2. How'd you get your start reading scripts?

For my first internship, I worked at a state film office that held an annual screenplay competition. They had an entire room stacked with feature-length screenplays, and it was my job to read and recommend scripts to the higher-ups for the contest. When I moved to L.A., I was able to parlay that experience into reading for a production company and then another screenplay competition, and it snowballed from there.

3. Is recognizing good writing something you think can be taught or learned?

I think anyone can be taught to do anything; whether or not they have a natural aptitude for it is another matter. The thing is, we are all storytellers. It's engrained in our psyche. And reading is a personal, subjective experience for each individual. Some stories that bore the pants of me might be endlessly entertaining to someone else, and vice versa. That's why a film can be rejected from one contest and then go on to win first place at another.

However, the technical aspects of a script can be judged in a fairly uniform way. Is the writing concise yet descriptive, or is it overly wordy? Are there misspellings and grammatical errors? Is the script formatted to industry standards? Is the page count a reasonable length? A writer can't control whether or not a particular reader will judge their writing as "good", but they can control the technical aspects of the script to give it the best possible chance of impressing a reader.

4. What are the components of a good script?

A good script has a solid premise, interesting characters, a well-conceived plot, tight narration and dialogue, and is technically up to par as far as typos, sentence structure, formatting, etc. It also must be ENTERTAINING. This is something I believe writers forget about sometimes, especially if they're writing, say, a historical drama. Audiences don't care about facts and figures and accuracy nearly to the extent that they want to have an emotional journey—a catharsis. It's the writer's job to provide that journey and entertain along the way—that's why we're in the Entertainment Industry. I think most readers would agree with me on this—the first question I ask myself after reading a script is, "Am I bored?" If I'm bored, then the script will not get a Consider or Recommend, no matter how true to life or historically accurate it is.

5. What are some of the most common mistakes you see?

By far, the most common mistake is spelling errors. Most scripts I read are chock-full of typos and glaring grammatical errors (including sentences with missing punctuation, missing words, or only parts of words.) It's incredibly frustrating because this is something completely under the writer's control. What writers may not realize is that every time I come across a typo, I'm taken out of the story. When a script has multiple typos per page, as some of them do, I'm taken out of the story dozens of times by the time I read the last page, which essentially ruins the experience. As writers, the written word is our only instrument. A pianist wouldn't perform on an out-of-tune piano, and likewise, a writer should fine-tune his or her instrument and become a master of language. Having a typo-free and correctly formatted script says to the world: "I'm a professional, and I care about the quality of my work." In my opinion, it's the best way to control your first impression to a reader.

6. What story tropes are you just tired of seeing?

There has been a trend over the past several years of incredibly brutal, violent, and bloody dramas. (And I'm not talking about horror movies here.) I think it's a reflection of the dark times we've gone through over the past decade and the current political landscape in the world. I've also programmed at some film festivals, and some films I screened were sickening to the point where I had to turn them off. I'm not a prude and I enjoy a good action or horror film just as much as the next person, but it's gone a bit overboard lately. Some of the films had gratuitous violence toward women and children, which I find disheartening and painful to read. Sometimes I long to read a comedy or something lighter that ends on a positive note, and I hope the trends change in the coming years toward lighter (and less barbaric) fare.

7. What are the 3 most important rules every writer should know?

1) Don't get disheartened if you aren't getting recommends or considers on your early scripts. Take the notes, learn from them, and keep writing. Your writing will improve greatly if you just keep at it.

2) It's okay to struggle with writing. Some writers get disheartened and give up if writing isn't the glorious, self-expressive, free experience they think it should be. Writing can be difficult and tedious. It's courageous to be vulnerable and put your heart out on the page, and even more courageous to then send your work to total strangers. The best thing a writer can do is show up every day and write, and when the work is ready, keep sending out those ships. One day, a ship will come back in.

3) You are in total control of your very first impression on the reader. You do so through your mastery of language, spelling, formatting, brief yet descriptive narration, etc. You can't control whether or not a reader loves your script, but you can control your presentation. Hire a professional coverage service to proofread and get feedback before you send your scripts out—it's the best way to test the waters and see how your script will be received, since many coverage services employ readers who have worked at contests and production companies.

Even if your script doesn't get a recommend, the writer themselves can. Scripts and writers are tracked by production companies, and if you as a writer make a bad impression, a company is less likely to be willing to read another one of your scripts. If you made a good impression as a writer but they just passed on that particular script, a company will be much more willing to read future work from you.

8. Have you ever read a script that was an absolute, without-a-doubt "recommend"? If so, could you give the logline?

Since most of my work deals with newer writers, I have not yet personally come across a script that was an absolute Recommend with no doubts in my mind. Most scripts I read have a solid concept but need work to get them industry-ready. I have read many scripts that I would recommend if the writer made adjustments and changes, and those scripts might receive a Consider.

9. How do you feel about screenwriting contests? Worth it or not?

Absolutely worth it. They're a great way to build up credibility and provide the 'pitching points' writers need to become interesting to agents, managers, production companies, etc. You don't have to win. Even being a quarter-finalist in larger contests or fellowships can make you attractive and garner interest in your work. And if you do win or place in a major contest, it can open doors for you very quickly if you take advantage of the opportunity.

Submitting to contests also provides built-in deadlines. If you know you have regular submission deadlines you have to meet, it puts a fire under you to write every day. It's not that expensive–you can take $400 and submit to most every major screenwriting competition and a couple of smaller ones. Think about all the things most people waste $400 on in a year (like coffee!). It's a small investment that can have a big payoff, if even just to get you motivated to write.

10. How can people can get in touch with you to find out more about the services you provide?

Go to ScriptReaderPro.com where you can check out our services or send me an email directly at info@scriptreaderpro.com FAO Rebecca.

11. Readers of this blog are more than familiar with my love/appreciation of pie. What's your favorite kind?

Pumpkin! I'm thrilled that it's Fall and we're just a few weeks away from Halloween, my favorite holiday. I'm going to have to binge on all the pumpkin products over the next couple of months before they're gone!

ABOUT THE AUTHOR

Justin Sloan is a writer at Telltale Games, as well as a screenwriter and novelist. Justin holds an MA in writing from the Johns Hopkins University and a certificate in screenwriting from the University of California, Los Angeles School of Theater, Film, and Television. In addition to his novels, he has published short stories and poetry, and his screenplays have won or placed well in such contests as ScriptVamp, TheGreenlight, PAGE, and the Austin Film Festival.

The above was accomplished while working first as a US Marine, then living abroad in Japan, Italy, and Korea through his first MA in international relations. Justin was a Presidential Management Fellow and a David L. Borne National Security Education Program scholar, among other non-writing related accomplishments. Justin knows about transitioning careers and understands what it is like to hunger for the life of a full-time writer; he was, after all, wooed away from international trade and international banking to his current position with Telltale Games.

For further writing by Justin, look up Telltale Games' *Game of Thrones* and *Tales from the Borderlands*. Justin's books (including audiobooks) can be found online, and reviews are always appreciated.

http://www.JustinMSloan.com

Additionally, some of the Podcasts in which Justin has been interviewed include:

- Veteran on the Move
- One Bold Move, Lead Like a Marine
- The Life After Military Service
- High Speed Low Drag (COMING SOON!)
- The Self Publishing Podcast

What next?

1) Sign up to follow Justin at **http://eepurl.com/bbpNjv** to learn about new publications and get freebies.

2) Check out other books in the Creative Mentor series, including *Military Veterans in Creative Careers.*